Bass
How to Play
Guitar

Easy to read • Easy to play
Basics, Styles & Techniques

Graeme Aymer & Alan Brown

D1601423

FLAME TREE
PUBLISHING

Publisher and Creative Director: Nick Wells
Project Editors: Sara Robson and Polly Prior
Consultant: Jake Jackson
New Photography: Stephen Feather
Art Director and Layout Design: Jake
Digital Design and Production: Chris Herbert

Special thanks to: Chelsea Edwards, Digby Smith and Catherine Taylor

10 12 14 13 11
1 3 5 7 9 10 8 6 4 2

This edition first published 2010 by
FLAME TREE PUBLISHING
Crabtree Hall, Crabtree Lane
Fulham, London SW6 6TY
United Kingdom

www.flametreepublishing.com

Flame Tree Publishing is part of The Foundry Creative Media Co. Ltd

© 2010 this edition The Foundry Creative Media Co. Ltd

ISBN 978-1-84786-702-5

A CIP record for this book is available from the British Library upon request.

Picture Credits
All photographs, diagrams and notation courtesy of Foundry Arts,
except the following: **Alamy:** Magnus Agren: 286–87; David Jones: 81;
Lebrecht Music and Arts Photo Library: 281, 285; Trinity Mirror/Mirrorpix: 283.
Getty Images: Richard Upper/Redferns: 289.

Printed in China

Contents

Introduction

'A chord is not a chord until the bass player
decides which note to play' Sting

There's magic in the bass. Its four giant strings offer
so much more power than the guitar and more flexibility
than the drums. Certainly, a great rock band needs a
fantastic guitar player, but without the underpinning
of a fabulous bass player, it's game, set and match.
And as for reggae, soul, jazz, just about any other
type of music, without bass, there is simply no music.

•

There are plenty of folk who choose the bass because 'it's
easier to play than the guitar'. Four strings vs six, after all.
In reality, any instrument is as easy or as difficult to play as
you make it. You can be 'Joe Root', playing the simplest lines
following the guitar chords slavishly, or you can aim to be a
Flea-like king of slap, re-channel the slippery melodic jazz
of Jaco Pastorius or strike the low-end left-field à la Sonic
Youth's Kim Gordon. It depends on what you want to do.

What will always help, however, is an understanding of
both music and your instrument. So, what do you need to
be a good bass player? There are two things. First, love the
instrument. Love the way it sounds when you play it, the
way it feels when you hold it, the quirks, nicks and knocks

it may acquire along the way, whether that's through gigging as you set out on your journey, or the occasional dent it gets in hobby use. It's not always love at first sight: so many bass players came to the instrument as a second choice, Paul McCartney and John Entwhistle among them.

Second, listen. Listen to other bass players live or recorded. More than that, though: listen to music. If you're playing with other musicians, listening to what they're doing, playing and saying will help your playing no end. Furthermore, listen to music from genres you think you don't like. You might learn more than you bargained for!

Oh, here's one more rule, and this is probably the most important of all: make sure you enjoy yourself!

Authors

Graeme Aymer (author) is a writer who fell in love with the electric bass in 1983 and has not looked back since, playing both professionally and for pleasure in a variety of projects and engagements. He currently lives in East London.

Alan Brown (musical examples) is a former member of the Scottish National Orchestra. He now works as a freelance musician, with several leading UK orchestras, and as a consultant in music and IT. Alan has had several compositions published, developed a set of music theory CD-Roms, co-written a series of Bass Guitar Examination Handbooks and worked on over 100 further titles.

1

2

3

4

5

6

7

8

9

10

11

12

1

Bass Basics

This chapter is your introduction to this illustrious world. You'll learn a bit about the bass and be introduced to all the parts of the instrument and shown how they function. We will then take you through a set of stretches designed to keep your arms and hands working properly before, during and after practice: bass playing is very physical. We'll also go over how to tune the bass and how to position your hands correctly in order to play.

RIGHT: Hofner 500/1 Violin Bass (1961).

1

Anatomy Of The Bass

The diagram on this page shows the main parts of the electric bass. For more explanation of the function of particular parts, see opposite.

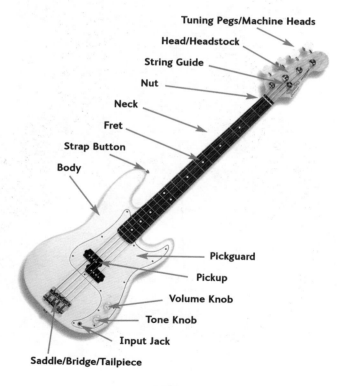

Tuning Pegs/Machine Heads

Head/Headstock

String Guide

Nut

Neck

Fret

Strap Button

Body

Pickguard

Pickup

Volume Knob

Tone Knob

Input Jack

Saddle/Bridge/Tailpiece

Tuning Pegs/Machine Heads: These control the pitch of your strings. These feature gears that make tuning up smooth and easy, and a groove holding the string secure.

Nut: This helps suspend the strings over the neck, together with the bridge, both of which will be discussed shortly. They can be made of brass, plastic or bone, each material affecting the tone slightly.

Neck: The neck is covered by the fretboard or fingerboard. This features 18–24 metal slats (frets) that define notes when the strings are pressed.

Pickups: These convert the physical vibration of the strings into electrical pulses for the amplifier. They can be active or passive: i.e. battery powered or not. A battery boosts power to the signal leaving the bass, so volume, bass or treble can be added using the control knobs (potentiometers) discussed in the pages that follow.

1

2

3

4

5

6

7

8

9

10

11

12

Bridge: This keeps the strings suspended above the neck and enables fine-tuning. It contains mechanisms to vary the height of strings above the frets (the action) and the length of the strings for accurate representation of notes (intonation).

Control Knobs: These are potentiometers, often referred to as 'pots'. They control the loudness of the bass (volume) and how much bass or treble is output (tone). Some basses use separate controls for each pickup while others combine functions, with a switch used to combine pickups or use each one separately.

Input Jack: This is where the bass is plugged into the amplifier.

Tip

Ask whether your bass is active or passive and find out how to change the battery if it's power assisted.

14

Truss Rods & Setting Up

One more thing. Inside your neck, there is something called a truss rod. It's a piece of metal that maintains the shape of the neck. Essentially, the strings and the neck form a shape a bit like a bow. Depending on temperature, heaviness of the strings, humidity and the material used to construct the neck, the bow can become more or less pronounced, which also affects the action and the ease with which you can play, as well as intonation.

When you buy a brand new bass, it's worth having your instrument 'set up'. An expert will check that the strings are the right height in relation to the neck, measuring and adjusting the action and intonation and that the truss rod is at the right tension. It will ensure your new

bass sounds as good as it can.

LEFT: Rickenbackers use a twin truss rod to support the long neck..

15

Getting Started

Practice makes perfect, the adage says. Practising is very important for musicians. Jeff Beck swears by it, and what's good enough for a legend like him is good for you as a beginner.

It's worth getting three pieces of equipment before you begin:

1. An electronic tuner, to make sure your strings are in tune.
2. A metronome of some sort to help you keep time accurately.
3. A small amplifier or something you can use to hear your bass when you are practising.

The great news is that these functions are often combined in a simple tool or software package. You can use Apple's Garageband if you use a Mac, for instance, using the drum loops to keep time,

LEFT: Electronic tuners like the Korg GA-30 will tell you instantly and automatically whether your strings are in tune, and are invaluable to musicians.

or many Zoom type pedals ship with tuners and drum patterns built in. The majority of electronic tuners also ship with metronome functions.

How long your sessions last depends on how much time you have. Some recommend spending an hour a day. What's more important is that you do it regularly. Spending at least five minutes doing some exercises every day is better than spending hours on the bass every few days. Try to give it a minimum of about 20 minutes every day. And have fun! Don't make it a chore.

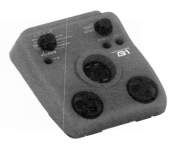

RIGHT: Multi-effects units like the Zoom B1 are moderately priced and feature a tuner, headphone output and rhythm tracks that will assist your practice sessions no end.

1

2

3

4

5

6

7

8

9

10

11

12

Warming Up Your Hands

Playing music is certainly spiritual and creative, but more than anything, it is physical. When you start out, your fingertips may become a sensitive for a short while until you get used to playing. Basses can be quite heavy, so if you're planning on standing or running around with one strapped to your person, you'll need a modicum of physical fitness.

Most of all, you'll be using the muscles in your forearms to pluck and fret four thick strings. For that reason, it's worth carrying out the following stretching exercises before each of your practice sessions. Doing so can also help you avoid cramps and pulls, and even more important, chronic problems like repetitive stress injuries.

18

STEP 1

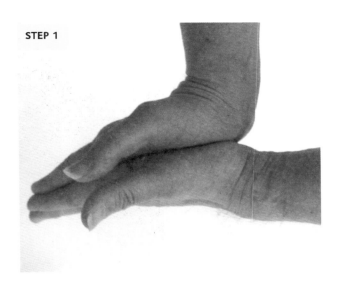

STEP 2

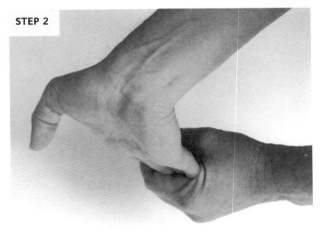

STEP 3

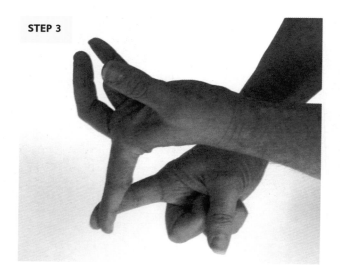

STEP 4

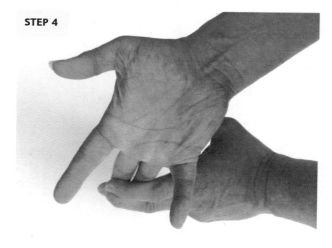

Tuning The Bass

There are four strings on a traditional electric
bass. From the fattest to the thinnest, they represent
the following notes: E, A, D, G. Sometimes they're
referred to as first string, second string, third string
and fourth string, with G as first, E as fourth.

It is vital that you keep your instrument in tune
when you're playing – ensuring that the note is not
too high or too low, even marginally. That will make
your playing sound bad, and clash with other
instruments if you're playing in a band.

The easiest way to find the right pitch is to use an
automatic electronic tuner. You plug it in and get a
reading instructing you to adjust your string tension.
However, it's important you learn how to listen to
your bass and tune by ear. It's easy to do this.

1

Exercise Steps

1. Find an instrument that is in tune, a tuning fork or a pitch pipe.

2. Play an 'A'.

3. Pluck the A string on your bass. Adjust it until it sounds the same pitch as the in-tune note.

4. Count five frets down the neck and press the A string down just behind the fifth fret. Play the note. It is a D. It should be exactly the same note as your D string, so you can tune that string.

5. Count five frets down the fingerboard and press the fifth fret at the D string. That's G. Tune the string using the machine head.

6. Press down the fifth fret on the E string. You should get an A, like the string you've just tuned. If not, tune your E string until the note at the fifth fret is the same as the A string.

7. Recheck all the tunings. The increased tension in the neck may have made your strings a little bit slack.

22

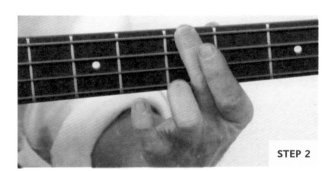

STEP 2

STEP 4

STEP 5

1

2

3

4

5

6

7

8

9

10

11

12

Tip

If you're having trouble deciding whether the string you're tuning is too loose or too tight compared to the in-tune note, hum the pitch of each string as you play. You'll hear the difference in your voice box.

ABOVE and LEFT: Tuners come in a range of handy electronic formats, from combination devices such as the Korg MA30 to apps on the Apple iPhone.

New Strings

You should replace your strings every so often: when you do so depends on how often and how hard you play. If you're practicing at home, that's probably once every six months or so, or every couple of months if you're gigging especially regularly. Strings pick up dirt and oil from your fingers and get dented and marked from smacking against frets, so their brightness diminishes over time.

ABOVE: Strings are sold according to the thickness or gauge, clearly marked on the packaging.

1

2 3 4 5 6 7 8 9 10 11 12

The first time you buy strings, you might be confused, as they don't usually feature the string names on the packaging. Strings tend to be sold by thickness, or gauge: light, medium or heavy. E strings will tend to be between 95–105 (which is actually 0.095–0.105 inches); A strings 75–85; D strings 55–65 and G strings 35–45.

Lighter strings enable faster movement, but can lack power and sustain. Heavy gauge strings are, predictably, the opposite. Medium can be a good compromise.

If you buy a set, you'll get quoted according to the gauge of the G string, for example: 'You want some 40s, mate?' Don't be afraid to try different sets until you're comfortable with the sound and feel.

Tip

Not all 40s are the same. Some manufacturers will use 75 and 95 gauge strings for A and E, while others will use 80 and 100.

26

Preparing To Play

Now that you know the parts of the bass and you're tuned up, you're nearly ready to begin your first exercises. Sit comfortably. Let's begin.

The Plucking Hand

Sit the bass on your leg. Rest your plucking hand (your right hand if you're right handed) very lightly

1

on the strings, with your thumb gently touching the E string. Try not to use the edge of the bass to support your upper arm (you risk cutting off blood flow to the hand) or resting the thumb too heavily on the pickup or E string.

Pluck the A string with your index finger, keeping the joint nearest the fingertip as firm as possible. Pluck the same string with your middle finger. Do the same with all the other strings, making sure your hand can reach all the strings evenly.

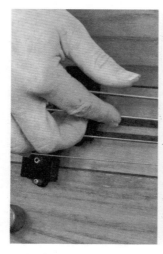
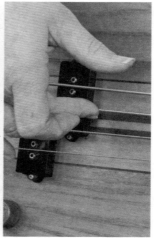

The Fretting Hand

Now it's time to use your fretting hand.

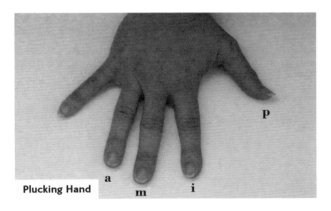

Plucking Hand

p

a

m

i

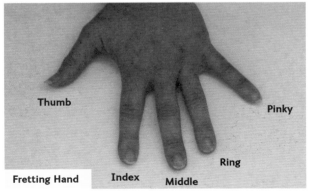

Thumb

Pinky

Ring

Fretting Hand

Index

Middle

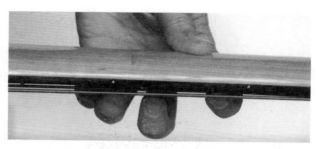

Gently hold the neck of the bass. Keep your thumb roughly in place behind your index and middle fingers.

Rest all your fingertips lightly on the E string. That is essentially the correct playing position for your fretting hand. Position your hand so that your pinky is just behind any fret and press down lightly. Sound a note with your plucking hand as per the previous instruction.

Using A Plectrum

Not all bass players use their fingers to pluck the
strings. Many of the best in the world use a plectrum
(or pick), like guitar players. Neither method is
better than the other.

The plectrum tends to add attack to notes, while
fingers have a warmer, softer, more rounded sound.
Plectrum playing is very common in rock music,

31

particularly among alternative musicians, but
also appears elsewhere; it's effectively used for the
O'Jays' funk classic 'For The Love Of Money' (1973).

Plectrum Technique

 To play bass using a plectrum:

Grip the plectrum between your index finger and
your thumb. Let the tip protrude slightly beyond,
just enough to be able to sound the string without
either becoming ensnared, or causing your
fingertips to rub on the strings themselves.

Hold it just tight enough that it won't fall out of
your fingers, but not so tightly that you get cramps
in your hand and forearm!

Try sounding the strings. Sounding the open strings
is fine for now. Just get used to playing 'downstrokes'
(striking the strings with a downward action) and
'upstrokes' (the reverse).

1

2
3
4
5
6
7
8
9
10
11
12

Exercises

When you're not holding down the strings to any frets, they're called 'open strings'. These exercises are for open strings, so just support the neck with your fretting hand for now.

Holding your bass in the position as indicated earlier, do the following:

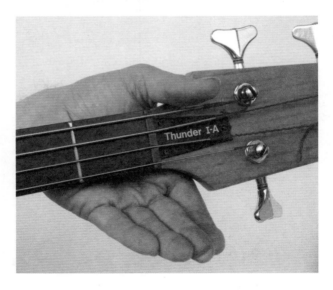

1

Count 'one, two, one, two' at a moderate and steady rhythm. Using your plucking hand, you're going to pluck with your index finger for each 'one' and with your middle finger for each 'two'.

You can do it with a plectrum, replacing your index finger with a downstroke and your middle finger with an upstroke.

Pluck each string four times according to the count.

1

Start with the E string, then move to the A and so on. When you've finished the G string, come back to the E via the D and A strings in the same manner.

Now, count 'two, one, two, one' and do the exercise again. (You should be starting with middle finger of the plucking hand.) Play from E string to G string and back to E string again. Concentrate on plucking the notes cleanly and at a steady rhythm.

2

Start Playing

So, now it's time to start playing. In this chapter, you will be introduced to the basics of fretting notes and some simple exercises to help with your positioning, endurance and technique. These exercises are, in fact, more than an introduction. They're designed to form part of every serious practice session you will have from here on in. If you spend 5–10 minutes a day working on the exercises in this chapter for all the years you play the bass, it will do you the world of good.

RIGHT: Yamaha BB414 (c. 2008).

2

Fretting

The most important thing to realize when playing notes on the electric bass is that you press slightly behind the fret to sound the note, not on top of the fret.

Try to keep all your fingers as close to the fingerboard as possible when you're playing. It's less tiring and it indicates better form. If you're fretting notes with your middle fingers, don't let your index finger point

ABOVE: Notice that the fingers are never far from the fretboard, and that notes are played by pressing down behind, not on top of, the frets.

40

2

in all different directions. Keep your ring and pinky as close to the neck as possible, too. This will give your hand less work to do and enable your playing to be much smoother. It may be a difficult habit to establish at first, but it is certainly worth cultivating.

When fretting, you want to be firm enough to make sure that the note sounds clearly, without excessive buzz and quick fading out (decay is the official term). However, don't press down too hard or else you risk cramp or worse, and your speed will be severely limited. A firm but light touch is best.

ABOVE: This is how not to do it!

Fretting Exercise

1. On the E string, pluck the open string (don't press any notes on the fretboard) in a cycle using your index finger and middle finger of your plucking hand. Count '1, 2, 1, 2' alternating between index and middle fingers. There's no rush: play as slowly as possible.

2. Using your fretting hand, press your index finger down just behind the first fret on the E string. Play the four-note cycle again, listening to make sure the note is clear and clean. Count '1, 2, 1, 2' again.

STEP 3

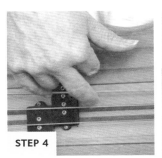

STEP 4

3. Next, use your middle finger to press down by
   the second fret. Repeat the exercise. Concentrate
   on making the notes sound cleanly.

4. Repeat the exercise using the ring finger behind
   the third fret, and then the pinky behind the
   fourth fret.

5. Reverse the exercises, pinky to ring finger to
   middle finger to index and finally open string.
   Repeat on the other strings.

Tip

Practice this exercise starting with the middle

finger too, counting '2, 1, 2, 1' and try

to play from open E to the fourth fret

on the G string without stopping

or using the same finger twice.

More Fretting Exercises

There are many more notes available to you than those you have been practicing so far. As you play with your fretting hand in different places on the neck, the distance between frets decreases, and may be easier to play if you have small hands. This exercise will help you explore those fretting opportunities.

STEP 1

1. Begin by repeating the previous exercise, fretting up to the fourth fret with your pinky on the E string and counting '1, 2, 1, 2'. Play the exercise on all the strings.

2. Now move your fretting hand along the E string so that the index finger can fret the note behind the fifth fret on the E string.

3. Play the note at the fifth fret with your index finger counting '1, 2, 1, 2'. Then fret the note at the sixth fret with your middle finger and repeat the count. Concentrate on keeping the form of your fretting hand and sounding the notes cleanly.

2

STEP 3

4. Repeat, using your ring finger at the seventh fret and your pinky at the eighth. Play and count just as before.

STEP 4

5. Repeat the exercise on the A, D and G strings.

6. Next, move your hand so that the index finger can play the note at the ninth fret on the E string. Repeat the exercise using your middle, ring and pinky fingers on tenth, eleventh and twelfth frets respectively.

STEP 6

7. Repeat the exercise from the ninth fret on the other strings.

Tip

If you are playing a series of notes right next to each other on the same string, it's called a chromatic progression.

46

Fretting & Damping

2

One of the toughest things in bass playing is preventing the bass from making unwanted noise. As you play one string, another may be sounding almost imperceptibly but just enough to interfere with the sound you're trying to make. The problem becomes particularly acute when you're trying to record the instrument. In that case, it's useful to become familiar with damping strings (stopping unwanted string vibration) as soon as possible.

The fretting hand is very important in terms of damping strings. However, the plucking hand has an important part to play and using it this way is a good habit to develop.

Damping Strings: Plucking Hand

1. Play any of the preceding exercises, as usual
   starting at the E string. Try not to rest your
   hand heavily on the pickup housing.

2. When you're playing on the A string, rest your
   thumb gently on top of the E string to prevent
   unwanted vibrating. Also, as your index and
   middle fingers pluck the A string, use the E
   string as a sort of buffer; the E string 'stops'
   the fingers from moving.

3. When you get to the D string, gently rest your thumb on the A string. Use some part of it to touch the E string, to prevent it from ringing quietly. Keep using the preceding string as a 'fingerstop' after you've played the note.

4. When you're playing on the G string, keep your non-plucking finger lightly on the D string to prevent it from ringing.

5. Repeat the other previous exercises practicing your right hand damping with each.

Concentrate on sounding the notes cleanly, rather than quickly. Damping is a combination of both hands. One more thing to bear in mind: make sure none of this becomes a chore. Have fun!

Damping Strings: Fretting Hand

Your fretting hand has a large part to play in the prevention of stray noise. It has a major part to play in note duration, for one thing, but by learning a few simple techniques and practices, you can keep your bass playing crisp and clean.

1. Play any of the exercises from earlier in the chapter.

2. When you're using your index finger at the first fret on the E string, lay the rest of your finger lightly across the other strings. Use your middle finger to help you press the note if you haven't developed the strength in your index finger.

3. When you're playing the note at the second fret using your middle finger, don't completely raise your index finger. Let it lie lightly across all the strings.

4. When you're playing the note at the third fret, don't completely raise the middle finger. Use it and the index finger to lightly touch the other strings.

1

2

3

4

5

6

7

8

9

10

11

12

5. Use a similar technique to play notes on the A string.

6. When you're playing notes on the D and G strings, lightly rest your index finger across the strings when you're using the other fingers, particularly the ring finger and pinky.

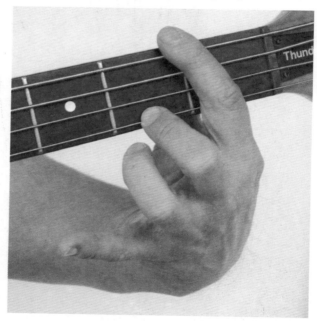

7. All the above applies when you're playing notes starting at the fifth and ninth frets.

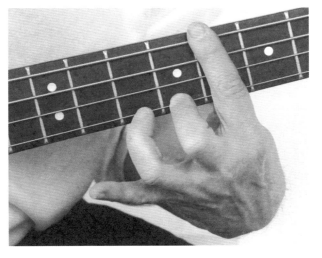

1

2

3

4

5

6

7

8

9

10

11

12

Damping With A Plectrum

Versatility is the name of the game in music, and
as such, it's worth thinking about playing exercises
for plectrum users. When it comes to using the
plectrum, your fretting technique won't change from
the exercises seen previously. Obviously, plucking
and damping will be different, however.

1. Hold the plectrum as demonstrated in Chapter 1.
2. Repeat any of the previous exercises using
   upstrokes and downstrokes rather than the index

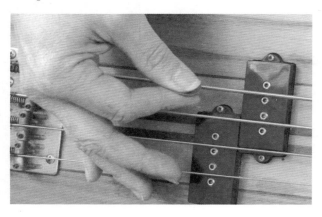

and middle fingers of the plucking hand, counting '1, 2, 1, 2'. Play slowly and concentrate on damping with your fretting hand, as previously shown.

2

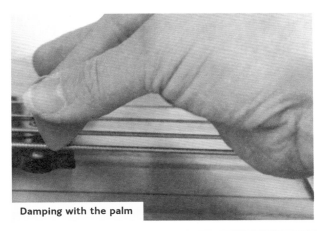

Damping with the palm

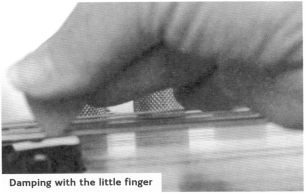

Damping with the little finger

3. When you have played the final notes in your cycle (played with the pinky), gently touch all the strings with the pinky on your plucking hand to stop the note from sounding.

4. Repeat the exercise in which you're playing from the fifth and seventh frets on page 45. While you're playing on the E and A strings, keep the pinky of your plucking hand gently touching the D and G strings to help prevent them from sounding. Use the fretting hand damping techniques from previous exercises.

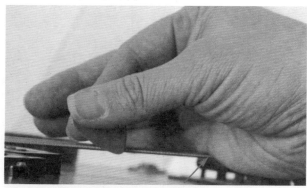

Damping with the palm on the string you're playing

5. When you're playing on the D and G strings,
lightly touch the E and A strings with any parts
of your plucking hand available, particularly
using the pad of the palm above the thumb.

Tip

**To damp strings, you can also use a thin wad
of sponge or similar material wedged under
the strings in the space adjacent to the bridge.
Beach Boys' bass player Carol Kaye swears
by this method!**

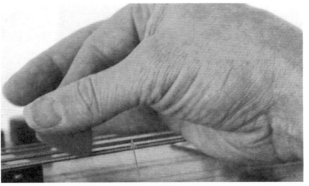

Damping with the little finger prevents buzz from other strings

1
2
3
4
5
6
7
8
9
10
11
12

3

Start Reading Music

If you take your music at all seriously, you should try to get to grips with some music theory. You needn't dive headfirst into complex notation, but for bass players, the fundamentals are valuable. With that in mind, this chapter aims to provide you with a basic level of music theory, including note names and values, time signatures and plenty about rhythm.

RIGHT: Yamaha RBX170 (c. 2005).

The Stave

The stave (sometimes called the staff) is fundamental to all music. It is the five lines and the four spaces that inform you of names of notes and how they should be played rhythmically. But the stave is nothing without a clef, a key to decode the pitch of notes to be played. There are four common clefs: treble, alto, tenor and bass. For the electric bass, you'll need to understand the bass clef.

Tip

Sometimes the bass clef is called the F clef. The curl of the symbol and the two dots surround the line that corresponds to the note 'F'.

In the bass clef, the notes in the spaces are, from bottom up, A, C, E and G. The lines correspond

Start Reading Music

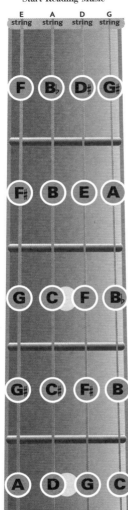

Tablature

For instruments like the electric bass, the stave has one disadvantage: it offers no clues about fingering. Guitar players and bass players often use the tablature system, usually in conjunction with the traditional stave.

The 'tab' has a representation of the strings as four lines; numbers show which strings should be played and which frets used. It is very useful and is an excellent aid to learning songs. It will be used in this book.

Types Of Notes

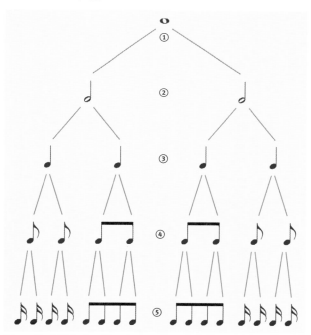

①	**Whole note**	Semibreve	4 beats in each bar
②	**Half notes**	Minims	2 beats in each bar
③	**Quarter notes**	Crotchets	1 beats in each bar
④	**Eighth notes**	Quavers	1/2 of a beat in each bar
⑤	**Sixteenth notes**	Semiquavers	1/4 of a beat in each bar

ABOVE: Notes are also defined by their 'beat value'.
Some last four beats, some two, some a fraction of a beat.

1

2

3

4

5

6

7

8

9

10

11

12

Sharps, Flats
& Naturals

Each note on the stave is separated by a distance called a tone or a whole step. So, it's a whole step from C to D or from G to A or from F to G, with two exceptions that we will see.

The halfway point is called a semitone or a half step. Sharps (♯) and flats (♭) refer to the halfway points between notes. On a piano, they're the black keys. A half step above a note is its sharp, while half step below is its flat. Again, there are two exceptions we're shortly to look at. Also note that G♯ and A♭ are the same note, as are D♯ and E♭ and so on.

Now, you might have a piece of music that always uses a sharp note: e.g., if you're playing in G major, you'll always need to play F♯ rather than F. However, in one or several passages in the music, the composer may wish you to play a straight F instead. That's called F natural (♮).

Remember when we said there are two notable exceptions? Here they are. The distance between B and C is only a semitone, as is the difference between E and F. There is no B♯/C♭ or E♯/F♭. Why that should be the case is far beyond the scope of this book. It's just one of those unfortunate rules.

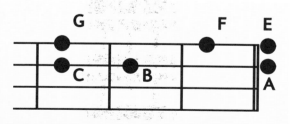

ABOVE: The fretboard showing interval differences.

Tip

An instruction in a piece of music to raise or lower a particular note with a flat, sharp or natural is called an accidental.

Exercise

RIGHT: Fill in the correct notes and the names for each position. Three notes have already been marked to help you start.

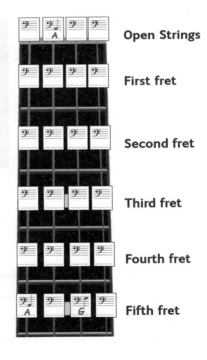

Open Strings

First fret

Second fret

Third fret

Fourth fret

Fifth fret

Dotted Notes

Sometimes you'll see a note with a dot next to it. That means you should extend its duration by half the value of the note. So, in the case of a minim, which lasts two beats, a dotted minim lasts three beats. A dotted crotchet lasts one-and-a-half beats, and so on.

ABOVE: A dot after a note means you should extend the duration by half the value of the note. Minim: worth two beats. Dotted minim: worth three beats. Crotchet: worth one beat. Dotted crotchet: worth one-and-a-half beats. Quaver: worth half a beat. Dotted quaver: worth three quarters of a beat.

Ties

Ties work similarly to dots. Two notes tied together have a beat value that is the sum of both their parts, e.g. two quavers tied together last for two beats.

69

1

2

3

4

5

6

7

8

9

10

11

12

They're often used to extend the duration of a note while preserving the beat count of the bar.

ABOVE: Tied notes can lengthen a note's duration while preserving the beat count of a bar, and ensuring that a piece of music feels like it's 'in rhythm'.

Triplets

For some compositions, you need to fit three notes into the space of two. This is the job of the triplet. Three notes will be grouped together and held together with what looks like a tie, bisected with a number '3'. You can count them as 'one-trip-let'. The key thing to remember with triplets is that they fit three notes into the space of two.

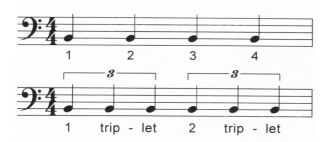

ABOVE: Triplets enable three notes to be played in the space of two, and have a particular rhythmic feel.

Rests

Sometimes it's not what you play: it's what you don't play. Rests tell you not to play, and how long not to play for. Just as there are beat values to types of notes, there are beat values for rests. They look like this:

Rest Values

Semibreve/Whole note rest: don't play for 4 beats

Minim/Half note rest: don't play for 2 beats

Crotchet/Quarter note rest: don't play for 1 beat

Quaver/Eight note rest: don't play for 1/2 a beat

Semiquaver/Sixteenth note rest: don't play for a 1/4 of a beat

Time Signature

Once you get past the clef at the beginning of the stave, you'll usually see either two numbers on top of each other, or something that looks like a letter 'c'. That is called the time signature and it tells you more about the overall rhythm of a piece of music.

Time signature is split into two numbers. The
number on top tells you how many beats there
are per bar, and the number beneath tells you what
kind of notes are being discussed. So,
for example, in a piece of music that is
$\frac{3}{4}$ there are three crotchets (quarter notes) per bar.
In $\frac{6}{8}$, there are six quavers (eighth notes).

In popular music, by far the most
common time signature is $\frac{4}{4}$; four
crotchets (quarter notes) per bar. This is referred
to as common time, and is often written as a C where
the time signature should be. A C with
a line through it is known as 'cut time',
$\frac{2}{2}$, which is uncommon in pop music
but tends to be used in classical music,
particularly for fast marching music.

Often, though not always, time signatures give a
piece of music a distinctive feel. For instance, $\frac{6}{8}$ will
be familiar to lovers of old soul classics
like Otis Redding's 'I've Been Loving You

73

So Long (I Don't Want To Stop Now)'. On the other hand, $\frac{3}{4}$ will be familiar to those who have watched anyone doing a waltz: hence its alternative name, waltz time.

More Time Signatures

There's more to time signatures than $\frac{4}{4}$, $\frac{3}{4}$ and $\frac{6}{8}$, however. Fans of bands like Soundgarden, Rush and early Genesis will find themselves contending with music written in time signatures such as $\frac{7}{4}$, $\frac{9}{4}$ and $\frac{5}{4}$, sometimes changing mid-song. In western music, those key signatures are considered to be on the experimental side. In other forms of music, particularly traditional music from Balkan states, however, there's nothing strange about music in $\frac{11}{4}$ time.

Without having the sheet music before your eyes, you just have to listen to the music and try to feel the beat instinctively. To clue you up about what to listen for, here are a few exercises.

1. Pink Floyd's song 'Money' is played mostly in
   $\frac{7}{4}$ time, though the saxophone solo is in $\frac{4}{4}$. Listen
   to the song, particularly the bass intro and see
   if you can count the 7-beat phrase. Try to get
   a feel for it.

2. Dave Brubeck's 'Take Five' is famously an
   experiment in $\frac{5}{4}$ time. Listen to the song
   and see if you can count the 5-beat phrase.

3. 'Synchronicity I' by The Police is written in
   $\frac{6}{4}$ time. Listen to it and see if you can feel the
   6-beat phrase.

Tapping Out Rhythms

Rhythm is pretty much a matter of working out how to count the duration of semibreves, minims, crotchets and the like. It's easy to learn and with a little bit of practice, it will become second nature.

The key is to sit down and count cycles of '1, 2, 3, 4' just as before. Get ready to tap your lap.

- To count semibreves, you'll tap your lap on the '1' of the cycle.
- To count minims, you'll tap your lap on the '1' and the '3' of the cycle.
- To count crotchets, you'll tap your lap on every beat.
- To count quavers, you do something different. You count '1 and 2 and 3 and four and ...' as a cycle and at the same speed as before. You'll tap your lap on every number and every 'and'.

76

- To count semiquavers, the common practice
  is to count '1-ee-and-a, 2-ee-and-a, 3-ee-and-a,
  4-ee-and-a …'. You tap your lap for every
  number, every 'ee', every 'and' and every 'a'.

Exercises

To play the following rhythms, count four by tapping
your foot, and then tap the written rhythm on a
tabletop or your lap with your hand. Count slowly
at first, but keep practising.

Rhythm Exercise 1

Rhythm Exercise 2

Rhythm Exercise 3

Basic Sight Reading

As mentioned earlier, being able to read music is a fantastic skill. There are plenty of musicians who have made a living without being able to read a note, but you'll have a far better vocabulary, be incredibly versatile and have an increased understanding of music if you can.

The following exercises are designed to get you on the road to reading music. If you have a friend that plays guitar or keyboards, they can play along with you, too.

'The Grand Old Duke Of York'

Start Reading Music

'Old MacDonald Had A Farm'

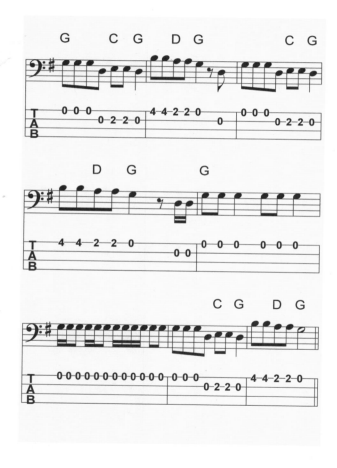

'Sing A Song Of Sixpence'

'Pop Goes The Weasel'

1
2
3
4
5
6
7
8
9
10
11
12

4

Scales & Chords

All songs are built on some kind of scale. Scales
are a palette of notes that go well together. There
are an infinite variety in use across the world, but
for the most part, western music consists of two
types of scales: the major and the minor scale. In
this chapter you'll learn what they are, how they
work, how to play them and how to practise them.
We'll also introduce key signatures and start you
on your way to understanding chords.

RIGHT: Fender Precision Bass (*c.* 2002).

88

Introduction To Scales

In the west, and in most of the music we will look at here, scales consist of a five-, six- or, most commonly, seven-note series.

The basis for our scale theory is the major scale. It will be familiar to you as the 'Doh, Ray, Me' song from *The Sound Of Music*: that song is an illustration of a major scale and handy to discuss as we go through. We tend to associate major scales with happy and bright, expectant or playful sound.

We will also look at minor scales. These tend to have a dolorous, sad, pondering feel to them. Many serious rock songs have a basis in minor scales.

What differentiate major and minor scales is the intervals between the notes.

Major Scale

The major scale is a series of seven notes; there is an eighth note, but it is the same as the first note (or root), but eight notes higher (one octave).

In the major scale, the distance between the first and second notes is a tone (whole step), between the second and third another tone, between the third and the fourth a semitone (half step), a tone from fifth to sixth and from sixth to seventh, and another semitone from the seventh to the octave. Think of it as tone, tone, semitone; tone, tone, tone, semitone.

ABOVE: This is the C major scale. On a piano, it corresponds to all the white notes. D and G open strings are played here.

91

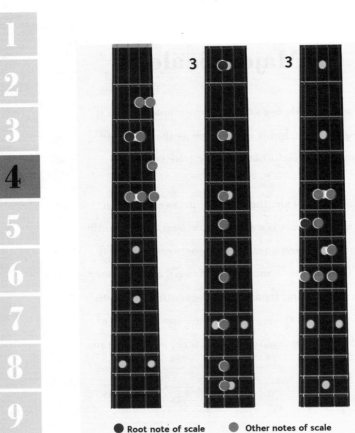

● Root note of scale　　● Other notes of scale

ABOVE: This is a C major scale for the bass. Try playing it now, and notice the distance between the whole and half steps between notes three and four, and between notes seven and eight. Try playing it in each of the fingerings shown here.

Natural Minor Scale

There are several types of minor scales, but to keep it simple here, we're concentrating on the natural minor scale.

In this scale, the interval between the first note and the second note is a tone, while there's a semitone between the second and third, and a tone between third and fourth, and fourth and fifth. Between fifth and sixth there's another semitone, with a tone separating seventh and octave.

ABOVE: This is the A natural minor scale. Try playing it now using the fingering charts shown. Note that starting from the note A on the piano, it also corresponds to all the white keys on the piano. That will become important later.

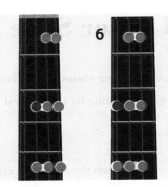

LEFT: Examples of fingering for the C natural minor scale. Remember that the intervals between third and fourth, and fifth and sixth are half steps.

Notice that A natural is the sixth note of the C major scale. Therefore, it is said to be the relative minor of C. Each major scale has a relative minor scale that starts on its sixth note.

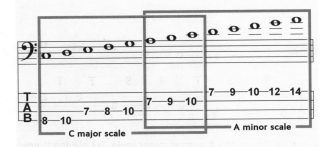

ABOVE: If you start the C major scale at the sixth note, A, you come up with the scale's relative minor. The same principle applies to any major scale.

Scale Exercises

When it comes to songwriting, coming up with bass
lines and undertaking any soloing, an understanding
of scales is invaluable. You can do all these things
by ear, or course, but having knowledge of how
the notes on the neck fit together will eliminate
much trial and error and open up your playing
to broad possibilities.

1. Try using the fingering charts on pages 92 and 94
   to play major and natural minor scales starting
   at notes other than C and A. In particular, try
   starting at G, D, F♯ and B.

2. Play the scales very slowly and call out the names
   of the notes as you play them. You could even try
   singing them along with your playing! Be mindful
   of when you use sharp or flat notes in any of
   the scales.

3. Try the F and B♭ major and minor scales, which start on the first frets of the E and A strings respectively. Write your own fingering chart in the spaces provided.

4. Try E and A major and natural minor scales starting at open E and open A respectively.

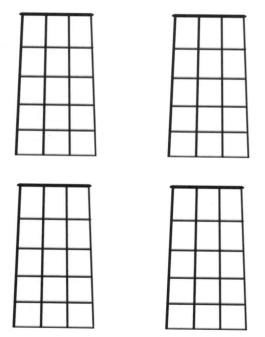

Again write your own fingering into the spaces
provided. You can check them against the
fingering charts at the end of the book.

5. Try to come up with your own fingering for playing
the major and natural minor scales using E♭ on D
string (first fret) and A♭ (first fret) on the G string.

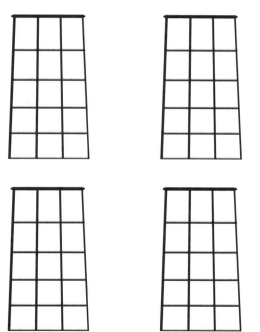

Key Signature

When you were playing the scales starting at different notes, you were introducing yourself to the concept of key signature. It's the final piece of the puzzle, and is something you'll see at the beginning of a piece of music, i.e. a number of sharps or flats.

Because of the configurations of half steps or whole steps required make sure a song sounds right, sharps and flats at the beginning of a piece of music instruct the players which notes should be raised or lowered. That is a key signature and they work like this.

C Major/A Minor

The intervals occur without the need to raise or lower any notes in the scale.

G Major/E Minor

F must be raised to F♯ to preserve interval between seventh and octave (or second and third notes for relative minor).

D Major/B Minor

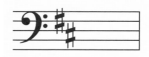

F is raised to F♯ to preserve interval between second and third (fourth and fifth in the relative minor) and C is raised to preserve interval between seventh and octave.

A Major/F♯ Minor

All the above remain true, while G is raised as the seventh note (or degree of the scale).

E Major/C♯ Minor

The above remain true while D is raised.

B Major/G♯ Minor

The above remain raised, while A is sharpened.

F♯ Major/D♯ Minor

Traditionally it's written as featuring six sharps, comprising all previously listed plus E♯. Remember, however, that E♯ is just F. It's semantics.

Circle Of Fifths

An easy way to visualize key signatures is by using the circle of fifths. The note going clockwise is always a fifth ahead; in the other direction, the next note is always four away. It's a handy tool to help you remember major scale key signatures and their relative minor scales.

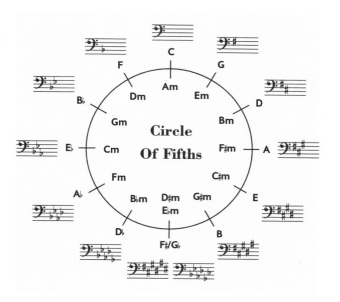

Triads

If you talk to guitarists, they'll often describe chords as being major or minor. The explanation of what makes a chord major or minor is actually very simple.

Chords have their basis in three notes along the scale: the first note, the third note and the fifth note. As there are three, this configuration is known as a triad. The distances between the notes in the triad are known as intervals. When it comes to triads, the most important interval is that between the first and third note. For a major chord, the distance between first and third notes is called a major third, with two tones (whole steps) between.

ABOVE: This is a C major triad, on the left, and the C minor triad on the right. Notice the major triad features an E, while the C minor triad features an E♭.

Minor chords have a flatted third. That is the distance between root and third is a tone plus a semitone (one whole step plus one half step).

There's one more thing. Bass players usually play chords as arpeggios: that is, they play individual notes in a chord separately rather than altogether as do guitar players or keyboardists. So, when you're playing your triads below, you'll be playing arpeggios.

C Major

C Minor

ABOVE: C major and C minor triads on the bass are shown here (the root note C is highlighted in blue). Notice the distance between the notes on fretboard in C major and C minor, in particular, from C to F and from C to F♭.

Scale & Triad Exercises

C Major & C Major Triad

Tip

This fingering is moveable for most

major scales.

G Major & G Major Triad

Tip

Use this as an alternative fingering

for major scales.

F♯ Minor Scale Exercise

Exercise 1

This first exercise ascends in the thirds; the second
descends in the sixths.

Exercise 2

Exercise 3

5

Further Scales & Arpeggios

It's time to go introduce modes. They may sound complex and theoretical but really they are simple, easy to understand and will open up your bass playing exponentially. We'll also look at seventh chords, so beloved of jazz and blues players, along with blues scales, and the funky pentatonic scales, major and minor. We will return to major and minor scales and see how to play them over two octaves.

RIGHT: Steinberger Headless Bass (1979).

Seventh Chords

Seventh chords build on the triads we looked at previously and they will add distinction and richness to your music. Understanding the seventh will mean that when a guitarist or keyboard player yells 'It's D minor seventh', during a rehearsal, you'll be able to play more than the D in the root. It's incredibly liberating and enlightening!

Major Seventh

One of the most 'jazzy' and relaxing sounding chords around is the major seventh. Take a major scale and play the first (root), third, fifth and seventh notes, and you'll get the major seventh arpeggio.

Exercise

Play the progression above, noting the way it sounds.

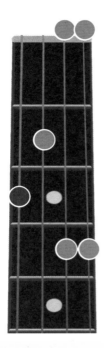

Gmaj7

ABOVE: The major seventh chord features root, major third, perfect fifth and natural seventh, all notes found in the major scale.

Minor Seventh

A minor seventh chord or arpeggio consists of root,
minor third, perfect fifth and flatted seventh, all
of which can be found in the natural minor scale.

Exercise

Play the progression above, noting the way
it sounds different from the major seventh
arpeggio played earlier.

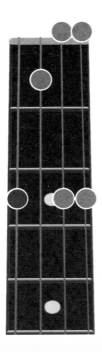

Gmin7

ABOVE: Notice the big difference between major and minor seventh. In this case, the B is flatted and F$_\natural$ rather than F$_\sharp$ is played.

More Seventh Chords

There are other variations of seventh chords worth knowing. Among them is the crucial dominant seventh. When you see a chord instruction for G7 or D7 chords, it refers to the dominant seventh, not the major seventh.

Dominant Seventh

The dominant seventh is similar to a major seventh, with its major third and perfect fifth intervals. However, a dominant seventh features a flatted seventh, like a minor seventh chord.

The dominant seventh is perhaps the most used chord in blues music and early rock'n'roll. It has many of the attributes of a major sounding chord or progression, but the flat seventh provides a great deal of tension and movement. There will be more on dominant sevenths when we come to examine major scale modes.

114

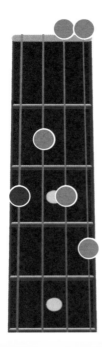

Gdom7

ABOVE: Notice that the dominant seventh chord is characterized by a major third but features a flatted seventh: the F is not raised.

Minor 7 Flat 5

This chord will also be referred to when we come to modes. The minor 7 flat 5 (m7♭5) does exactly what it says on the tin. It is exactly like the minor seventh we looked at earlier with one significant difference: rather than a perfect fifth, it features a flatted fifth.

In terms of sound quality it's not especially dissonant, but with prudent use it will add pleasant tension and movement to a composition. Note that the m7♭5 is sometimes referred to as a half diminished chord.

Exercise

Play the progression opposite, noting the way in which its sound differs from the major seventh and minor seventh arpeggios played earlier.

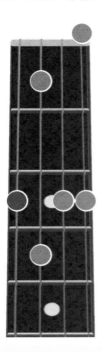

Gm7♭5

ABOVE: Notice that the m7♭5 chord is characterized by a flatted fifth, along with its flatted third and seventh.

Diminished Chord

The diminished chord features the minor third
and the flat fifth, but as for the seventh, it is
flatted twice.

Exercise 1

Play both of the exercises on pages 120–21 at
steady tempo. The speed at which you play them
doesn't matter. Play the first progression noting
the way in which its sound differs from the major
seventh and minor seventh arpeggios played earlier.

Exercise 2

Play the second progression just concentrating
on hearing the notes, understanding what you
play and keeping the tempo steady.

118

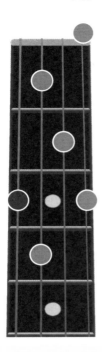

Gdim

ABOVE: Notice that the F in the G diminished chord is
flatted, effectively becoming E. In a true G minor scale,
the sixth note would be $E_\flat$, so in effect, the double flat
is like a raised sixth.

1

2

3

4

5

6

7

8

9

10

11

12

Diminished Exercise 1

Diminished Exercise 2

1
2
3
4
5
6
7
8
9
10
11
12

Introducing Modes

Modes are simply another way of looking at the
major scale. You start and end at a different root
note, but you keep all the notes and intervals of
the scale intact.

There are seven in total all and each has a name
based on the Greek music history. To explain better,
how they work, we will examine the C major scale.

Root: Ionian Mode

Sticking with the C major scale with which we're so
familiar, we will begin with the Ionian mode. This is
simply the original scale itself, no variation, no fuss.

122

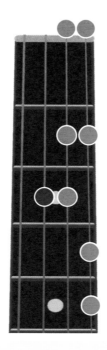

Ionian Mode

ABOVE: The Ionian mode starts on the root note of the scale, in this case, C major.

1
2
3
4
5
6
7
8
9
10
11
12

Second Degree: Dorian Mode

Dorian mode is simply what you get when you begin playing a major scale starting at its second note: D. So, if we decided to play D Dorian, we would simply be playing a C major scale starting at the second note, ending with the second note one octave up.

By nature it's a version of a minor scale. There is a minor third, a perfect fifth and a flatted seventh. Unlike a natural minor scale, however, there is a whole step between the fifth and sixth notes on the scale. This gives Dorian progressions minor chord gravity with something of the brightness of a major scale. Famously, Bernard Edwards' riff for Chic's 'Good Times' is simply a funky Dorian progression.

Second fret

5

Dorian Mode

ABOVE: Notice that the D Dorian is simply playing a
C major scale but starting and ending at D.

1
2
3
4
5
6
7
8
9
10
11
12

Third Degree:
Phrygian Mode

If you continue the exercise and start on the
E (the third note in a C major scale) you end up
with the distinctive Phrygian mode. Again, it's a
minor scale, with its minor third, perfect fifth and
flat seven. What sets it apart is that the interval
between the Phrygian root and the second note is
merely half a step: a semitone. This gives this mode
an almost Indian or Middle Eastern feel but is often
used in jazz and flamenco music.

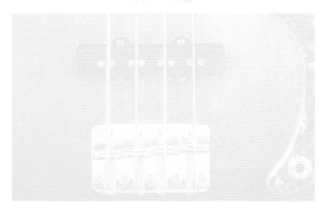

Sixth fret

Phrygian Mode

ABOVE: Notice that the E Phrygian is simply playing a
C major scale but starting and ending at E.

Fourth Degree: Lydian Mode

Start a major scale at its fourth note and you'll get the Lydian mode. Unlike the two preceding modes, Lydian progressions are characteristically major scales. That is, between root and third there are two whole steps, a perfect fifth and a raised seventh.

The mode is set apart, however. This is due to the presence of a raised fourth: a whole step between the third and fourth notes, rather than a half step, as is the case for a true major scale. For lack of a better description, this gives Lydian progressions a spacey, airy feel. Listen to the bass progression on the Police's 'Every Little Thing She Does Is Magic' is based on a Lydian phrase. Similarly, REM's 'Man In The Moon' also uses Lydian phrasing in the verses.

to the notes G, B, D, F and A. There are several mnemonic devices employed to memorize these. For the space notes, many people use the sentence 'All Cows Eat Grass'. For the line notes, there's 'Good Boys Deserve Food Always' or the snappy 'Great Big Dogs From Africa'. Find and remember one that works for you.

A   C   E   G   G   B   D   F   A

ABOVE: If a note to be played is outside the range of those on the stave, ledger lines may be used.

ledger line

A   B   C   D   E   F   G   G   F   E   D   C   B

ABOVE: When the notes used are beyond the five lines of the stave, ledger lines are used. When the line goes straight through the note, it becomes a line note. When it is above or below the note, it is a space note.

Stave & Fretboard

It is useful to see how the notes on the stave relate
to the notes on your instrument's neck. The open
strings (below) are E, A, D and G. By pressing
your finger on each fret on each string the sound
and therefore the note changes. The diagram
opposite shows you all the notes.

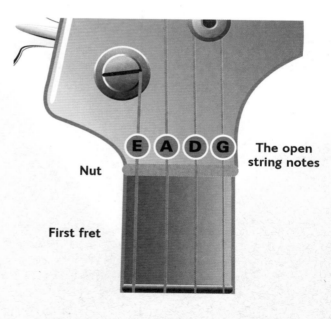

Nut

First fret

The open
string notes

Sixth fret

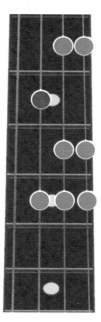

Lydian Mode

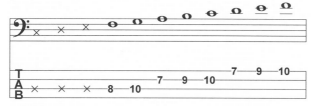

ABOVE: Notice that the F Lydian is simply playing a
C major scale but starting and ending at F.

Fifth Degree: Mixolydian Mode

This is, perhaps, the king of the modes. The fifth degree of the scale is called the dominant. This should help you to understand the relationship between this mode and the dominant seventh chord we looked at earlier.

Like the Lydian mode, the Mixolydian is also a major scale progression, with a major third and perfect fifth. However, it features a flatted seventh.

You'll notice that if you create a triad of this mode and add the seventh, you get the dominant seventh chord, as we discussed earlier. The dominant seventh chord is used extensively in blues and rock'n'roll records: think Bill Haley's 'Rock Around The Clock' or Little Richard's 'Lucille'.

Ninth fret

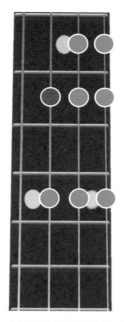

Mixolydian Mode

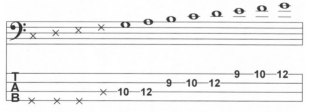

ABOVE: Notice that the G Mixolydian is simply playing a
C major scale but starting and ending at G.

Sixth Degree:
Aeolian Mode

Whenever we've discussed a major scale's relative minor, we've been secretly talking about the Aeolian mode. Start a C major scale at A, and you'll get A natural minor, or A Aeolian. You know how it sounds and how to play it.

Here are a few interesting observations about the Aeolian mode, however. It is also used extensively with blues and rock songs; it means you can sometimes play notes in the associated major scale to rock songs based on Aeolian progressions, as long as you resolve them cleverly enough. So, you could play, say, a C major triad or C major seventh in a song primarily in A natural minor, but you'd want to come back to A.

That is, end your phrase at the Aeolian root, rather than that of the major scale.

Ninth fret

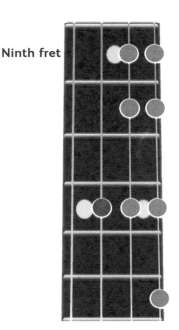

Aeolian Mode

ABOVE: Remember that A Aeolian is simply playing a
C major scale but starting and ending at A.

Seventh Degree:
Locrian Mode

The Locrian mode is the strangest of the modes,
featuring both a flat second note and a flat five.
Otherwise, it features a minor scale's flat third
and minor seventh.

Interestingly, if you take the first, third, fifth
and seventh notes in the scale, you end up with
a m7♭5 chord.

Locrian Mode

ABOVE: Notice that the B Locrian features a flatted second, third, sixth and seventh. It is simply playing a C major scale but starting and ending at B.

Exercises In Modes & Sevenths

Play the following exercises at a leisurely but steady, consistent pace. Make: sure you heed the key signatures.

D Dorian With 7th Arpeggios & Alternative Fingerings

E Phrygian With 7th Arpeggios
& Alternative Fingerings

5

F Lydian & 7th Arpeggios
With Alternative Fingerings

G Mixolydian With 7th Arpeggios

A Aeolian Scale
& 7th Arpeggios

B Locrian Scale

B Locrian 7th Arpeggios

Mode & Arpeggio Exercise 1

Mode & Arpeggio Exercise 2

1
2
3
4
5
6
7
8
9
10
11
12

Pentatonic & Blues Scales

Not all scales consist of eight notes. There is such
a thing as the pentatonic scale, so named because
it only consists of five notes. For our purposes,
we'll say that there are two kinds of pentatonic
scales: major and minor.

A great deal of rock music is based on the minor
pentatonic scale, as it's a variant of the natural
minor scale. The major pentatonic scale appears
in a lot of poppier Motown music.

Major Pentatonic Scale

We'll start by examining the major pentatonic scale.
Simply put, it is a major scale that omits the fourth
and seventh notes. In C, that means playing C, D, E,
G and A. This yields a very happy and incredibly
versatile, moveable progression.

142

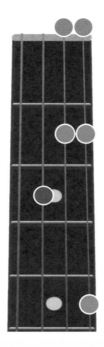

C Major Pentatonic Scale

```
T                           0     2     5
A            0     2
B     3
```

ABOVE: A simple first position C major pentatonic scale.

1
2
3
4
5
6
7
8
9
10
11
12

Minor Pentatonic Scale

Similarly, the minor pentatonic scale is a natural
minor scale with two notes missing. However, it is
the second and sixth notes in this case. Hence, in
an A minor pentatonic, you'd play A, C, D, E and G.

Exercise

**Play the progression indicated in the following
chart and try to keep a rhythm as you play.**

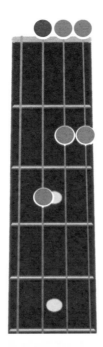

5

A Minor Pentatonic Scale

ABOVE: A simple first position A minor pentatonic scale.

1
2
3
4
5
6
7
8
9
10
11
12

Blues Scale

The blues scale is a six-note scale variation of the minor pentatonic. The difference is that you add a flatted fifth between the fourth and fifth notes.

The minor pentatonic and blues scales are used extensively for guitar solos in rock music, so, as previously stated, you probably know exactly how they sound. Angus Young from AC/DC is perhaps one of the most well-known adherents of such pentatonic playing. There's nothing wrong with that, of course!

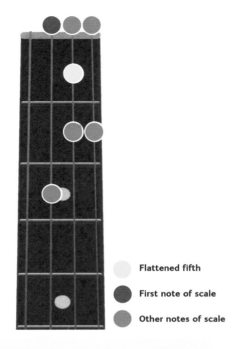

Flattened fifth

First note of scale

Other notes of scale

A Blues Scale

ABOVE: The blues scale is identical to the minor pentatonic scale, except for a flatted fifth in between the fourth and fifth degrees.

Exercises

Fill in the missing notes in the following scales:

Major Pentatonic Scales

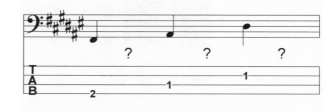

Minor Pentatonic Scales

5

Blues Scales

Further Scales & Arpeggios

Assorted Scales

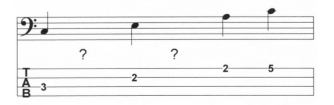

Scales Over 12 Frets

There's a saying that musicians use sometimes: don't let your instrument control you. Make sure you control your instrument. This means that you become so familiar with it that playing new things, making new things up on the spot and playing with others becomes easy and second nature.

One way to do this is to learn to play your major and minor scales over two octaves. The following diagrams show suggested fingerings for scales across the 12 frets from the nut, indicating playable notes in the same scale before the first root where a two octave range extends above the 12th fret.

Exercise

When you practise playing your scales in this way, call out the notes – it will help you become familiar with which notes belong in which scales.

152

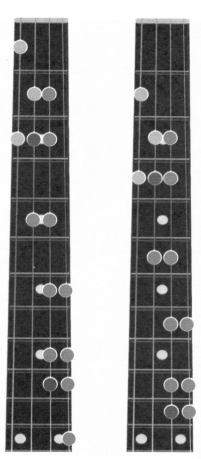

C Major   **C♯ Major**
Fingering diagram of major scales over twelve frets
● Root note   ● Scale notes   ● Scale notes before first root

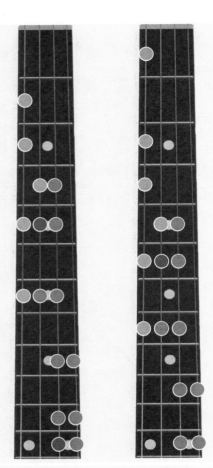

D Major   **E♭ Major**
Fingering diagram of major scales over twelve frets
● Root note ● Scale notes ● Scale notes before first root

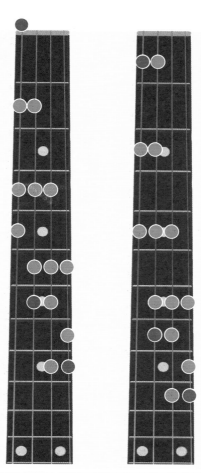

Further Scales & Arpeggios

E Major   F Major

Fingering diagram of major scales over two octaves

● Root note ● Scale notes ● Scale notes before first root

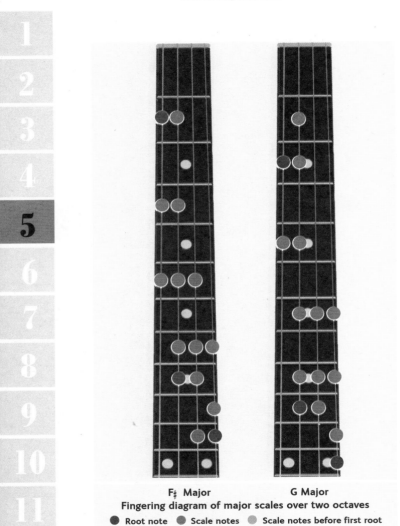

F♯ Major   **G Major**
Fingering diagram of major scales over two octaves
● Root note ● Scale notes ● Scale notes before first root

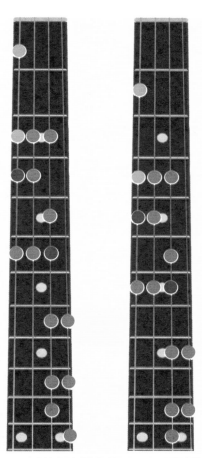

A♭ Major   A Major
Fingering diagram of major scales over twelve frets
● Root note ● Scale notes ● Scale notes before first root

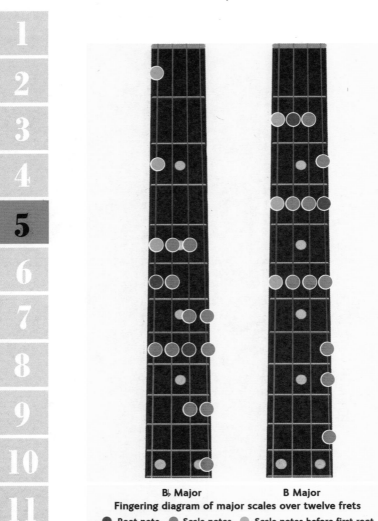

B♭ Major   **B Major**
Fingering diagram of major scales over twelve frets
● Root note ● Scale notes ● Scale notes before first root

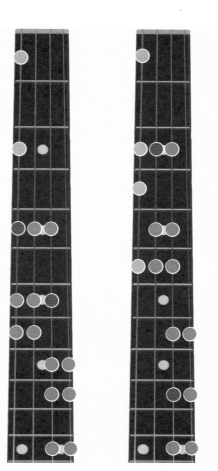

A Minor   **C Minor**
Fingering diagram of minor scales over twelve frets
● Root note ● Scale notes ● Scale notes before first root

A Major Pentatonic   C Major Pentatonic
Fingering diagram of major pentatonic scales over twelve frets
● Root note   ● Scale notes   ● Scale notes before first root

A Minor Pentatonic   C Minor Pentatonic
Fingering diagram of minor pentatonic scales over twelve frets
● Root note ● Scale notes ● Scale notes before first root

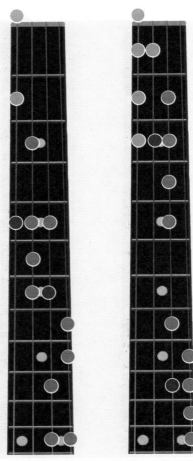

A Blues Scale **C Blues Scale**
Fingering diagram of blues scales over twelve frets
● Root note ● Scale notes ● Scale notes before first root

Seventh Arpeggios Along The Major Scale

Practise your major scales, playing the seventh arpeggio of each degree of the scale. Refer to the earlier description on Modes (pages 122–35) if you need help constructing each arpeggio. For example, for C major, play the C major seventh arpeggio (**first** degree of the scale, or Ionian), followed by the D minor seventh arpeggio (**second** degree, or Dorian) the E minor arpeggio (**third** degree, or Phrygian), the F major seventh arpeggio (**fourth** degree, or Lydian) and so on.

Major Scale Arpeggio Exercises

Practise your major scale arpeggios using as few hand positions as possible. The fingering charts on the next two pages will guide you. We will work up the degrees of the G Major scale.

163

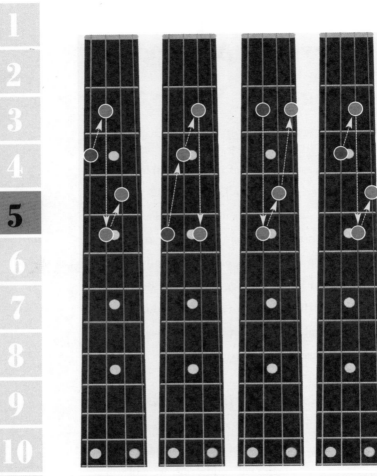

G Major 7th   A Minor 7th   B Minor   C Major 7th
Ionian   Dorian   Phrygian   Lydian

Fixed position 7ths for arpeggios in G Major.

D Dom 7th   E Minor 7th   F♯ Minor 7th flat 5   G Major 7th
Mixolydian   Aeolian   Locrian   Ionian

Fixed position 7ths for arpeggios in G Major.

Exercises In Further Scales & Arpeggios

'Motown Shuffle'

'Stax Boogie'

'Kool Groove'

'Dominants Boogie'

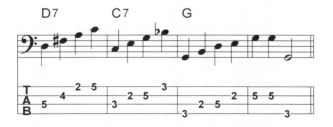

'Smooth Sheep'

Further Scales & Arpeggios

171

1
2
3
4
5
6
7
8
9
10
11
12

6

Creative Bass Playing

In this chapter, we will look at how chord progressions follow one another, what tension and anticipation mean in music, and the importance of melody and harmony. Then we'll delve into the characteristics of different genres of music, from the blues to calypso, just so you'll have a flavour of playing a range of types.

RIGHT: Westone Thunder II (1983).

172

Tension, Anticipation & Resolution

Music and storytelling share a need for tension and movement. You need a bit of both to create something that's gripping and feels like it's going somewhere.

In music, tension, anticipation and resolution can be driven by many mechanisms including rhythm, harmony (including disharmony), volume, tempo and chord progression.

For the bass player coming into an already written song, rhythm is very important. In a run of indie rock quavers, for instance, resting for one or two can make a huge difference in terms of how the song sounds. There's a huge change mid-song in the middle of 'How Soon Is Now' by The Smiths. Notice how much the feel of the song differs between the two sections.

Tension Exercise 1

Tension Exercise 2

Tension Exercise 3

Note Progression

Composers often talk about resolution when it comes to notes and chords. That is, there's a pull towards the root, note or chord one (indicated by a Roman I) in the scale. So, for a song in C major, all other chords have a tension against C and the C major chord. Some notes and chords have a real need to get back to the I, in particular, the IV and the V. They are the three chords in so-called three-chord rock'n'roll and are the backbone of such songs as Eddie Cochrane's 'C'mon Everybody', Ritchie Valens' 'La Bamba' and Richard Berry's 'Louie Louie'.

Bass players sometimes use a similar device to keep their bass lines moving. In country, Latin and some Caribbean and African music, for instance, bass players sometimes drop or rise to the fifth of whatever note they're playing to maintain a song's momentum.

178

'Back To My Roots'

'Up Country'

'Calabaza'

Groove

What is groove? Well, it's bit like trying to describe what a colour looks like: you know it when you see it. That said, groove very often involves an element of repetition and an element of syncopation, i.e. playing 'off the beat'. In $\frac{4}{4}$ music, beats 1 and 3 tend to be the most important. When you're syncopating, you're emphasizing any other beat, particularly the 'ands' between the beats. Grooves work very well with:

1. Short repeated phrases: live loops, in effect.
2. Locking the bass notes tightly to the rhythm of the bass drum.
3. Playing short notes.

Also, if you're heavily syncopating your bass notes, it's useful to 'come back to the one' to cite Bootsy Collins, every two to four bars or so. It prevents the listener from becoming lost, and it also builds tension as you wait for that resolution.

Passing Notes

Another way to raise tension and inject the
unexpected into your bass playing is to include
'wrong notes'. For instance, if you're about to play
the root to a C chord, you could fleetingly play a B
for the first half of the beat, 'passing' over it to the
C. You could similarly pass the other way through
a C♯. As long as you use such notes sparingly and
wisely, and as long it's appropriate to the type of
music you're playing, passing notes will add tension
and an interesting off-kilter feel to your music.

Listening Exercise

Listen to James Brown's 'Give It Up Or Turn
It Loose', (with Bootsy on the bass) and note
the relationship between the bass and the drums.
Also notice how much of the playing is between
the beats, but it always comes back to the 'one'.

Now try a few examples of groove playing for yourself along with the exercises below.

Groove Exercise 1

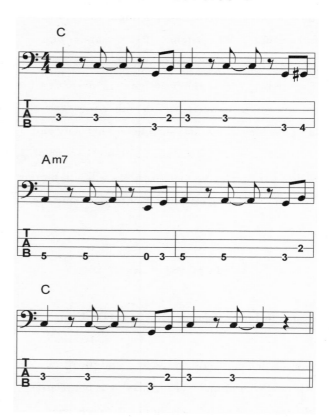

Groove Exercise 2

Groove Exercise 3

Groove Exercise 4

Walking Bass Lines

There are two ways to think about walking bass lines. One way is that virtually every note of the bass line is a completely different note based on the piano or guitar chord used. That's how a lot of traditional jazz works but is used by rock musicians too. It's featured prominently in Van Morrison's 'Moondance'. Former Pretenders' bass player the late Pete Farndon also uses the technique on the song 'Message Of Love'.

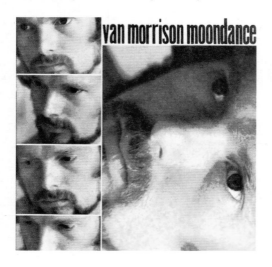

This technique draws on the bass player's knowledge of modes and arpeggios; that is, you'll understand what notes can be used with a D7, a G major, an A minor 7 and so on. Mixing this technique with passing notes as previously discussed is extremely effective.

You can also 'walk to a note'. This is a case of playing a three-, four- or five-note chromatic progression at the end of the bar preceding. Larry Graham uses this technique in the bass line for Sly and the Family Stone's 'Dance To The Music'.

6

Walking Bass Exercise 1

Walking Bass Exercise 2

Walking Bass Exercise 3

Walking Bass Exercise 4

1
2
3
4
5
6
7
8
9
10
11
12

Melodic Playing

Related to walking bass lines is melodic playing.
The theory is the same: you understand the arpeggios
that outline whatever chord is being played, but you
use your bass line as a counter melody to what's
being sung or played on another instrument.

Paul McCartney is very effective at using this
technique. It's apparent on songs like The Beatles'

194

'Penny Lane', 'Rain' and 'She Said She Said'. It's also evident on several Wings' tracks, in particular, 'Silly Love Songs'.

Rock players should look to the Smiths' Andy Rourke for the perfect example of how to execute this technique. Particularly in 'This Charming Man', he demonstrates perfectly how to combine melodic bass playing and walking the bass in a rock setting.

Also consider traditional reggae music in which almost all the bass lines are counter melodies to the singing. Listen to Aston 'Family Man' Barrett's playing on Bob Marley and the Wailers' track 'Zimbabwe' for an example of this.

Exercises

Consider the melodies on the following pages.
Play along with the straight versions, then play
the alternative bass lines as examples of
melodic and walking possibilities.

'She'll Be Coming Round The Mountain'

'She'll Be Coming...'
(Take Two)

'She'll Be Coming...'
(Take Three)

'Polly, Put The Kettle On'

'Polly...' (Take Two)

'Polly...' (Take Three)

1
2
3
4
5
6
7
8
9
10
11
12

Rock Music Bass Lines

Rock music is a strange term. Rock includes everyone
from U2 to Judas Priest, and you'd agree that these two
bands don't share many similarities. But in rock music,
you will tend to find that many tracks do two things.

First, the root note of whatever the guitarist is
playing will become the bass line. Your job as bass
player is to reinforce the guitar, both for rhythm
and chord progression.

Second, if the guitar rhythm becomes spaced out,
you may be required to keep the song's drive through
the use of straight quavers. Listen to AC/DC's 'You
Shook Me All Night Long' and Nirvana's 'In Bloom'
as examples.

Exercise 1
Play along to these rock type bass lines.

Rock Bass Line 1

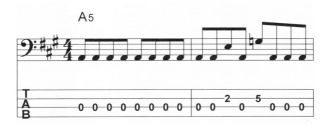

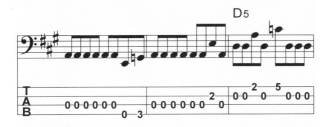

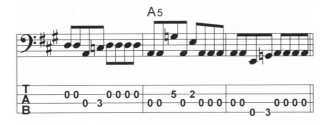

Rock Bass Line 2

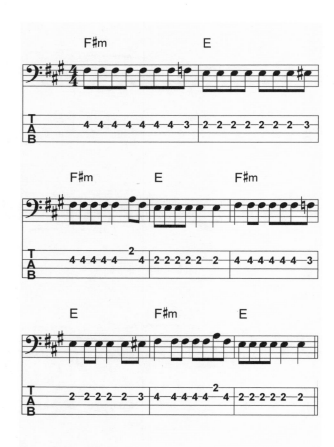

Rock Bass Line 3

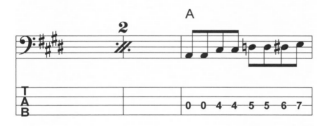

Exercise 2

Of course, there are plenty of pentatonic scales used in rock music. Glen Matlock's bass playing on 'Anarchy In The UK' touches on major pentatonic scales, while much of The Who's John Entwistle's playing uses major and minor pentatonic scales. Here are two rocky pentatonic scales.

Rock Bass Line 4

Rock Bass Line 5

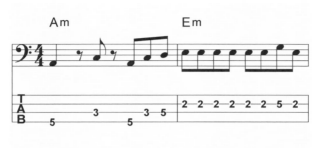

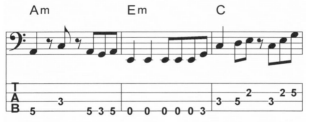

1
2
3
4
5
6
7
8
9
10
11
12

Blues & Rock'n'Roll

If you understand the blues, you'll understand rock'n'roll. In fact, the examples below will follow the traditional 12-bar blues cycle, used by much early rock'n'roll. For those based on dominant seventh chords, you can use Mixolydian-style progressions. Some are more minor pentatonic, and blues scale based, with which you can use natural minor (Aeolian) progressions.

Exercise

Play along with the blues and rock'n'roll examples on the pages that follow.

Bluesy Bass Line 1

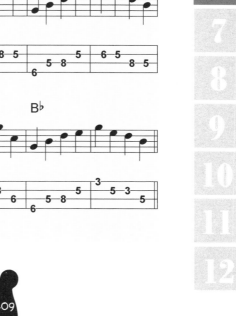

Bluesy Bass Line 2

Bluesy Bass Line 3

Jazz

Jazz is steeped in mystique. Many rockers regard jazz players as overly intricate, while some jazz players equate rock music with a lack of sophistication.

Whatever the case, the good news is that if you have followed the earlier section on modes, you have everything you'll need for basic jazz playing. Use your arpeggios and modes to walk your bass lines through the chords and you'll manage just fine.

Exercise
Play along with the jazz examples
on the following pages.

Jazz Bass Line 1

Jazz Bass Line 2

Jazz Bass Line 3

Soul

Just as rock is a broad term, so too is soul. Motown music from the 1960s was very bright and poppy, while in the 1970s, post Marvin Gaye's *What's Going On* album, it became far more gritty. Stax's soul roster, with backing from the MGs was an entirely different flavour altogether.

Exercise

The following exercises provide a flavour of this era of soul.

Soul Bass Line 1

Soul Bass Line 2

Soul Bass Line 3

Funk

Why funk is so-called is anybody's question.
However, a funky bass line will often, though
not always, feature a fair amount of syncopated
movement between the root and the flat seventh.
The tempo is often just slow enough to enable the
music to swing, but quick enough to encourage
dancing. In fact, with funk, if people are dancing
to your bass playing, you're doing it right!

Exercise
**The following exercises are designed
to get you thinking funky.**

Funk Bass Line 1

Funk Bass Line 2

Funk Bass Line 3

Disco

Disco was the dance music of the 1970s. It was
a simple, sped-up type of 'funk lite' for those who
couldn't quite understand the heavy syncopation
of funk, and who were dancing to music in the
new institution, the discotheque. If there's one
bass playing device that screams 'disco!' it is the
modulation between root and octave. A slow version
of this bass line is Lipps Inc's 'Funky Town', while
a more sped up version might be Sylvester's 'Mighty
Real'. Faster funk lines would often work as disco
bass lines, however.

Exercise

The following exercises are designed to
illustrate the disco-style bass playing.

Disco Bass Line 1

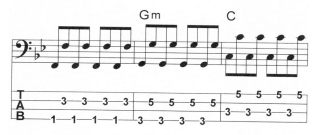

Disco Bass Line 2

Disco Bass Line 3

Hip-Hop

Again, it's difficult to characterize hip-hop bass
playing; sampling means that if you have a good idea
of any of the above styles, you're well on your way.
However, be clear on one thing. Playing hip-hop
bass is about restraint. Most important in hip-hop
is definitely the beat, the drums. You might play
a very short phrase at the beginning of the piece
but it will be extremely minimal, perhaps a couple
of notes every two-to-four beats. This is no absolute
rule, but do bear it in mind if you find yourself
a hip-hop gig.

Exercise

**Listen to 'Empire State Of Mind' by Jay-Z,
The Fugees' 'The Score', and 'Ms Fat Booty'
by Mos Def for more ideas on hip-hop
bass playing.**

228

Hip-Hop Bass Line

Country

As mentioned previously, traditional country music bass players will move between the root and fifth of the chord they're accompanying (or, they modulate between I and V). Sometimes they play the V below the I, sometimes above, depending on the range of the instrument. It's a simple device, but if you're playing a lot of it, and you're playing relatively fast, you'll need to concentrate because it's easy to slip up. With the sparseness of the music, if you lose track, your mistake will stand out.

Have a listen to 'Folsom Prison Blues' or 'San Quentin' by Johnny Cash (or most Johnny Cash from that era) for inspiration.

Exercise

Play along with these country examples.

Country Bass Line 1

Country Bass Line 2

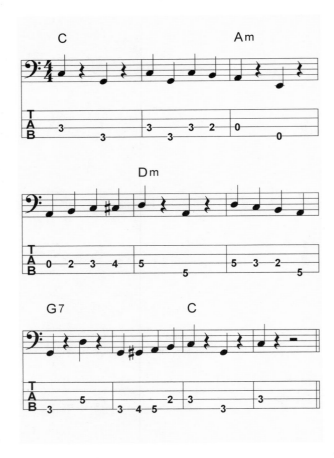

Country Bass Line 3

Reggae

Reggae, even more than funk, relies on the bass line. In traditional roots reggae, the singer will usually carry a melody, while the bass will use a repeating countermelody phrase. The other instruments may have some melodic frills, but much of what they're doing will be concerned with rhythm.

Here's another thing peculiar to traditional, or roots, reggae. Whereas in funk the one is the most important beat, in reggae, it is the three. It is called, as Bob Marley described in his song of the same name, the 'One Drop'. 'Slavery Days' by Burning Spear is the perfect example of this. Through the 1980s, it's fair to say that reggae took on a more American structure, including a funk-influenced element, with the one becoming more important. But the three remained important. In particular, check out some Sly & Robbie, particularly their work with Black Uhuru. A good example is 'Guess Who's Coming To Dinner'.

234

Reggae Bass Line 1

Reggae Bass Line 2

Reggae Bass Line 3

1
2
3
4
5
6
7
8
9
10
11
12

Calypso & Salsa

Like country music, these Caribbean-derived musical flavours use a lot of root (I) and fifth (V) playing. But there are differences. Traditional calypso often moves V-I, on a pair of quavers (eighth notes) at the second and fourth beats. The bass lines often join in with various melodic phrases throughout the song.

Latin music, particularly Cuban salsa rhythms sees the bass line coming in halfway between the second and third beats, and resolving on the fourth. Similarly, the bass often plays melodic phrases in unison with the rest of the instruments during select parts of the song.

Exercise

Play along with these examples of Caribbean music.

238

Calypso Bass Line 1

Calypso Bass Line 2

Salsa Bass Line

7

Advanced Techniques

In this chapter, you'll find out how to play the slap and pop technique made famous by Red Hot Chili Peppers' bassist Flea. If you want to play notes even beyond the range of the guitar, you can actually do that on the bass thanks to a little something called harmonics. And then, of course, you can play more than one note at a time, with what's known as doublestops and by playing chords on the bass. It's all there, and it's all here, so read on.

RIGHT: Warwick Streamer LX (1996).

242

Slapping & Popping

Supposedly it was Sly And The Family Stone bass player Larry Graham who was credited with inventing the slap and pop style on electric bass. He says he did it because he was playing with his mother in church and there was no drummer, so he started 'thumping' the bass to compensate. It's simple to do. First we'll look at the slap.

The Slap

You're going to be hitting your E, A and D strings with the final knuckle of your thumb, the one closest the nail. Hold your plucking hand so your thumb is parallel with the strings. Then, flick your wrist so that the knuckle hits the E string cleanly, being sure to damp the unplayed strings with your fretting hand. You should be striking the string around the spot where the fretboard meets the body.

244

The Pop

When you're feeling comfortable with that, you can try popping. Your plucking hand should still be in the position shown in the previous image. Now use your index finger to pull on the G string and let it snap back, as if you were gently pulling the string on a bow to shoot an arrow. Try to pop a few clean notes on the G and D strings and gradually become comfortable with the technique.

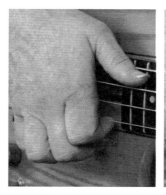 

ABOVE LEFT: The Slap, with the knuckle of the thumb.
ABOVE RIGHT: The Pop, the index finger pulling off the G string.

Combining Slap & Pop

Now we'll combine the two techniques. With the
thumb, slap the F at the first fret on the E string.
Then pop the F one octave away, the third fret on the
D string. Slap the G (E string, third fret) and pop G
(fifth fret D string). Slowly continue this way, playing
the F major scale, slapping on the E and A strings,
and popping on the D and G strings. Keep it slow
to begin with, and then keep practising, gradually
increasing your speed over the next few weeks.

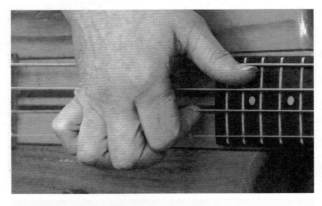

ABOVE: The Slap, with a Pop on the D string.

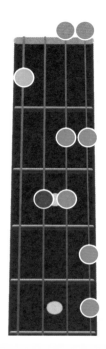

5

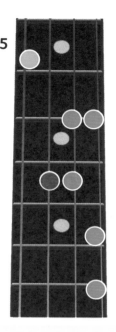

Slap & Pop Scale

ABOVE: A slap and pop scale in F major. Note that the
thumb and index finger follow separate scales.

Exercise

To build up your ability to slap and pop,
try to play the following passages.

3 Pop & Slap Bass Lines

Fretting Hand
In Slap & Pop

Slapping and popping is usually considered a
plucking hand technique, but you can use your
fretting hand to add to the effect.

The Hammer-On

You don't have to use your plucking hand every
time you want to sound a note. Sometimes you can
use your fretting hand to sound a note, to hammer-
on. Try these two ideas.

Slap a G note on the E string (third fret), using your
fretting hand's index finger to hold the G down.
While the note is still sounding, bring your pinky
into place fairly forcefully to fret an A (fifth fret).
You don't need to use your plucking hand again.

Try it slowly at first, gradually getting faster.
Try similar things on the A, and even the D string.

Now, pop a B♭ on the G string (third fret), using
your index finger to fret the note. While the note
is sounding, bring down your pinky fairly forcefully
to sound the C (fifth fret). No need to pop the string
with your fretting hand for that exercise.

One more thing to try. Slap a C on the A string
(third fret). Then pop the B♭ on the G string (third
fret). Then hammer-on the C on the G string (fifth
fret). Play slowly until you can build up your speed.
It should sound pretty funky!

Hammering-on C

1
2
3
4
5
6
7
8
9
10
11
12

Fretting-Hand Slap & Pop

With left-hand slap and pop, the idea is to not sound notes; you damp all the strings so you turn the bass into a kind of drum.

It works like this: rest your fretting hand lightly across the strings. Raise all your fingers except your index. You'll be using it to mute all the strings. Do this around the third or fifth fret.

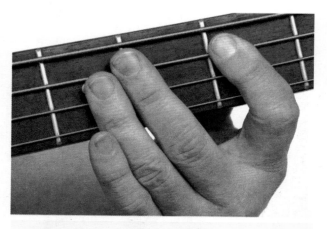

ABOVE: The fretting hand is used to make a percussive thud.

Use your thumb to slap the E string. You should get a muted 'thud'. Then hit the strings with the rest of the fingers on your fretting hand, not hard enough to produce a note, just enough to produce a similar thud to thumb slap. It won't be as loud, but if you're using an amplifier, it will have enough of an effect. Now repeat both steps.

Now we'll add a pop...

Do as you did before, using the thumb to slap the E string and the fretting hand fingers to echo the thump. But instead of going back to the thumb, use your plucking hand's index finger to pop a muted note on the D string. Then use your fretting hand's free fingers once again to hit the strings. After this, slap the muted E string and repeat the exercise, starting slowly but gradually working up your speed.

In fact, you can use your fretting hand just to mute all the strings, so you end up with interesting percussive patterns mixed into your clear slapping and popping.

Exercise

Play the following passages slowly at first,
and gradually speed up over time, when you feel
comfortable playing in this style. If you see a
note with an 'x' for a head, that means mute the
note (a ghost note). If they're close together, use
the fretting hand slap.

3 Slap & Pop Bass Lines

255

1
2
3
4
5
6
7
8
9
10
11
12

Harmonics

A strange thing happens when you pluck a bass string. It actually vibrates at a series of mathematically related frequencies. The loudest, of course, sounds like the note you've played, but there are several higher notes also sounding.

Those higher notes are called harmonics. There's a way to hear them clearly, which reveals a chiming, bell-like sound.

Natural Harmonics

You can only do this exercise on open strings. Start with your E string. Touch it very lightly with your index finger directly above the fifth fret. Now, pluck the string, but just as you're plucking the string, lift your fretting finger fractionally afterwards. You should hear a chime-like ringing of an E note. Do the same at the seventh fret (producing a B),

256

the ninth fret (producing A♭) and the twelfth (another E). Repeat using all the strings. Work out what notes you're hearing.

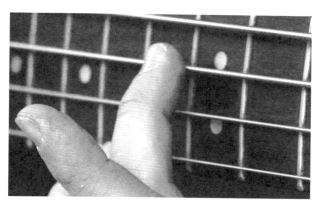

ABOVE: When playing a natural harmonic, it is important not to press down on the fret in question, but lightly touch the string.

Tip

The harmonic note at the fifth fret of any bass string is exactly the same as the harmonic note at the seventh fret of the thinner string next to it. You can use this knowledge to tune up your bass.

Bassist Jeff Ament uses harmonics played on a
12-string bass to get the loud, chiming sounds in
the introduction to the song 'Jeremy' by Pearl Jam.

False Harmonics

You can trick your bass into thinking that a fretted
note is an open string, however. Doing so invokes
what is known as false harmonics. If you know what
you're doing, you can get some incredibly interesting
effects. Jaco Pastorius, whom some call the greatest
bass player who ever lived, used all false harmonics
on the bass to provide the guitar-esque opening to

ABOVE: The finger plucks while the thumb gently rests on the
fretted string.

the famous Weather Report song 'Birdland'. On
his first solo album, his track 'Portrait Of Tracy' is
similarly reliant on false harmonics to mesmerizing
effect. You'd do well listening to both tracks.

Be warned: it's not easy. It takes practice to get
any precision and consistency.

Fret a C on your G string (fifth fret), but don't
actually pluck the note. Instead, hold your plucking
hand open-palmed over the strings, above your
pickups. Next, stretch your thumb out and lightly
touch the string as close to the place where the neck
meets the body as possible.

7

Now pluck the string with your middle finger; if you
have a bit of fingernail, try to use that. You should
hear a chiming note.

Move your plucking hand up and down the string
all the while holding down the fifth fret. Notice the
nature of the notes.

Doublestops & Chords

Playing chords on the bass can often end up in a murky, muddy-sounding mess. The most common chord shapes played on the bass are usually the tenth, major and minor, and the fifth chord.

The former is simply playing **7** a third above a root, but rather than playing a couple of frets away, which yields the aforementioned muddled sound, you play the third

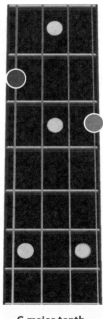

C major
tenth   C minor
tenth

C major tenth

one octave higher. You'll end up with something that sounds like playing the third an octave above your root, i.e. the tenth, sounds far more palatable. It will remind you of Herbie Flowers' famous bass line for Lou Reed's 'Walk On The Wild Side', although that song is played with two basses.

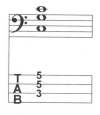

The fifth chord on the bass simply involves playing an octave together, inserting a fifth between. It's the equivalent of a power chord that guitar players might use. Listen to 'Sacred Love' by the Bad Brains, in which bassist Darryl Jennifer uses fifth chords to emphasize the power chords being played by guitarist Dr Know.

Tip

If you plan to use the fifth a lot, try turning
down some of the bass in your tone.
It will sound quite muddy otherwise.

261

8

Playing With Others

Unless your bass playing ambition goes no further than playing a lot of scales in your bedroom, you're going to want to play with others at some point in your life. This chapter is all about that. It's about how to approach the bass, playing with others and soloing, and equally important, how to choose gear that will help get your sound out there, from amps and speaker cabinets to home recording software and signal processing plug-ins. Read on.

RIGHT: Fender Jaguar (c. 2006).

262

8

Choosing Your Gear

Selecting Your Amp

An electric bass player needs an amplifier, or amp.
If you're planning to join a band, you'll need one with
enough power to provide you with a clear, punchy
sound without needing so much volume that it distorts
(starts to sound fuzzy). You should be able to hear
yourself comfortably, without being forced you to
play really hard, risking strain or other injury. How
powerful that is depends on where you'll be using it.

LEFT: This unit features a
head, and a single cabinet.
Many cabinets feature
only one kind of speaker,
often four 10-inch (25-cm)
speakers. For small halls and
stages, this will suffice if the
amp is sufficiently powerful.

Choosing an amp is about getting the power, sound, cost and portability right in relation to your needs. How are you getting from gig to gig? Do you have a

ABOVE: This unit features a head, and a single cabinet. Many cabinets feature only one kind of speaker, often four 10-inch (25-cm) speakers. For small halls and stages, this will suffice if the amp is sufficiently powerful.

ABOVE: This unit features a head, and a single cabinet.
Many cabinets feature only one kind of speaker, often
four 10-inch (25-cm) speakers. For small halls and stages,
this will suffice if the amp is sufficiently powerful.

car or are you using public transport? Do you have a big car? Are you playing in pubs or in church or a youth club? Do you have £200 to spend or £2000?

For most small hall and small club situations, a bass amp between 100–400W will likely be fine. If you're going to play rock music at local live venues, go for 200W+. It won't matter whether you use an all-in-one combined (combo) unit or one in which the head (amplifier's electronics) and cabinet (the speaker housing) are separate. That will depend on transport. If you're big and strong and have a spacious car, then this is no issue.

But do find the sturdiest unit you can afford. Bass speakers vibrate a lot, and as such will need to use good quality, solid materials to deliver the best sound. In addition, your speaker cabinet should be enclosed, not open-back like a guitar amp. Consider buying a less powerful but better built system rather than a more powerful one of cheaper construction.

8

Signal Processing Equipment

Compressors

On stage and in the studio, you may want to try using a bit of compression on the bass. Some basses sound very loud when a note is plucked, (attack) and allow notes to fade very quickly (decay). A compressor will even out some of those attack and decay issues. Using too much compression will, however, detract from the natural sound of your bass, so be careful with the effect.

Attack and decay issues are very noticeable when recording. Most music recording software will ship with software compression functions or plug-ins included. However, compression is processor-intensive, so it's not a bad idea to buy a hardware unit if you can afford it.

LEFT: Compressors iron out noise peaks and troughs particularly noticeable in recordings. Floor pedals are effective, but for home recording, a small, desktop unit may provide more control and precision.

Limiters

A limiter is like a compressor that only activates when it hears a certain volume being exceeded. Many bass amplifiers come with built-in limiters. In fact, you'll likely see a lot of units and software around that is sold as 'Compressor/Limiter'. For playing live, limiters will help you avoid clipping, or the distortion (fuzz) that comes from the bass being too loud for the amplifier to handle.

8

269

Equalizers

There are two types of equalization (EQ): graphic and parametric. Graphic equalization is very broad, acting as a series of volume knobs or sliders for specific frequency ranges. Parametric is far more specific, and will enable you to tweak very specific characteristics

ABOVE: Software parametric equalizers feature far more advanced sonic tools that take practice to perfect.

of a frequency. Most amps will ship with a graphic equalizer built-in. Parametric EQ is usually more of a studio issue, and as such, most decent music recording software will feature parametric EQ plug-ins and functions. Note that using parametric EQ effectively takes a lot of practice.

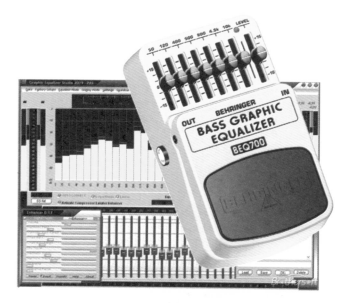

ABOVE: The graphic equalizer, in either software or foot pedal form features a series of sliders that control frequency volumes.

271

Phase Shifters, Choruses

& Flangers

The phase shifter adds a very swirling sound to the signal, somewhat similar to a Lesley organ speaker. The chorus roughly mimics the effect of having several instruments playing together. It's very noticeably used during the introduction of Krist Novoselic's bass introduction to Nirvana's 'Come

As You Are'. A flanger is something of a mix of the two. It can produce a sound similar to Graham Coxon's swirling noise in the guitar part for Blur's 'Girls And Boys'. These effects can sometimes

remove bottom end, so look out for units specific to bass. (Vintage effects often produce far better sounds, but can cost a lot more.)

Distortion

The staple pedal for all rock guitarists, the ever-present distortion pedal can be interesting for bass players too. Larry Graham uses a lot of fuzz on many Sly and the Family Stone tracks. Using a touch of the right distortion can also warm up a sterile sound, particularly rolling off all or most of the treble. Use with care, as they can rob you of bottom end. Look for bass-specific effects.

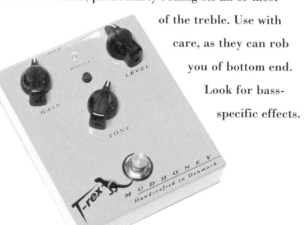

8

273

Octave Dividers

These units split your signal, mixing your original sound with one that is one octave lower. They can be highly effective in funk playing, or, with a distortion pedal for rock.

Whammy Pedal

Whammy pedals are very flashy kit. They're a bit like reverse octave dividers, enabling you to create notes very much higher sound than whatever you're playing. They're fairly expensive and highly conspicuous, so handle with care.

Wah-Wah & Autowah

Jimi Hendrix showed the world just what wah-wah could do to guitar on the intro to his track 'Voodoo Chile (Slight Return)'. Autowah applies a similar effect automatically to every note you play. Yesteryear's units used to rob bass players of low end, but these days, there are more around with bass in mind. They're a lot of fun.

8

Digital Delay & Loop Stations

Digital delay is also known as the echo box. You can set them to give you just a hint of reverb, to simulate playing in a large hall, or cavernous echo, as if you were playing in the Alps. Loop stations enable you to set musical phrases to repeat ad infinitum while you play other lines or solos. Bass and reverb don't really mix, but you can do very interesting things with echo, particularly if you're slapping. Similarly,

loop stations will have very limited use in a band, but you could use one on solo performances or for very specific songs or song parts.

Multi-Effects Units

Newer, programmable effects units like the Zoom
B1 and B2 combine many of the above effects and
a whole lot more. They're relatively inexpensive and
are quite a lot of fun. Also, they double up as tuners
and usually feature headphone sockets and drum
loops, so they're handy for practising. If you can
afford one, buy one.

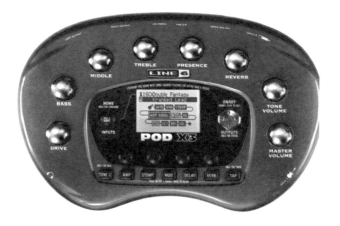

8

277

1
2
3
4
5
6
7
8
9
10
11
12

Tip

Digital effects eat batteries.
If you buy one, make sure you get
a mains power supply as well.

Digital Audio Workstation

This is your music recording software. There
are a great deal on the market, from the freebie
Garageband to high end ProTools. Choose one that
has a light version, but also has an upgrade path.

If you find yourself
taking recording very
seriously in a couple
of years, it will be
cheaper to get the
next version up,
and easier to learn
the more feature-
laden edition.

278

The wide range of available software includes Cubase (FAR LEFT), MULAB (TOP), Garageband (CENTRE) and Logic Express (LEFT).

8

1
2
3
4
5
6
7
8
9
10
11
12

In Praise Of Simplicity

The best way to learn how to play bass is to play with others, full stop. Suddenly you'll find out about technique from other musicians you meet, new ways of thinking from those you're playing with, and be forced to improve to keep up.

Now, unless your band is a Squarepusher-like (a.k.a. Tom Jenkinson) concept involving hours of bass solos, you'll also have to 'unlearn' to play. By unlearn, the idea is that, you might know all your modes and be able to play wonderful Dorian mode licks and perfected your slapping and popping, but those techniques may not suit the song.

If your singer is singing a tender song about love and loss and you start slapping up your bass, chances are

RIGHT: Bassist Mike Herrera and guitarist Tom Wisniewski of American pop-punk band MxPx.

you're not adding anything to the song. Don't play any more than the song needs. The backing band needs to do just that: back. Don't detract from whatever the song is about. Simplicity usually works best.

1
2
3
4
5
6
7
8
9
10
11
12

Playing With Drummers

Bass players and drummers are traditionally known as the rhythm section. You two are responsible for setting the rhythmic tone, the drive and the punch of the music. Listen to the drummer, who should in turn listen to you. Things will usually go well if you listen to the bass drum and try to keep with its feel and rhythm. You don't necessarily have to lock to what the bass drum is doing, but suit what it's doing in your playing.

Mike Mills plays a wonderful line in REM's song 'Radio Free Europe'. During the verses, Mills and drummer Bill Berry maintain a very standard crotchet (quarter note) pulse, but in the bridges (between verses and choruses) Mills plays a melodic counter rhythm that works incredibly well. It's well worth a listen.

282

ABOVE: Bass player Sting and drummer Stewart Copeland combine to form the rhythm section of The Police.

283

Playing With Guitarists

With guitar players, you'll always have to bear in mind space. If you're in a rock band with one guitar player and no other instruments, you will have more space to express yourself as a bass player, to make sure you keep the sound filled up. If there are two or more guitar players, you really will have to keep your general playing simple, or else you'll all be falling over yourselves trying to eke out a bit of space. That's not necessarily a limiting factor, of course. For example, rather than sticking to root notes of chords, mix them up with thirds or fifths or sixths for a bit of variety. But whatever you do, play like a bass player and not a frustrated guitar player! Keep the bottom end and keep the rhythm.

RIGHT: Thin Lizzy's Phil Lynott showing us that bassists can still take centre stage.

284

Playing With Keyboardists

What applies to playing with guitar players also applies to playing with keyboardists. Be very careful of clutter. There is one extra factor to take into account with keyboards, though. Keyboard lines,

286

particularly those played by trained pianists, will have a left hand part, the hand with which they play their bass parts. Listen out to make sure they're not encroaching on your territory, that the keyboard bass isn't in your sonic space, or else you'll end up with a low-end muddle. Make sure you're both playing with each other, and not against each other.

BELOW: UK alternative rock band, White Lies.

8

Playing With Singers

Without a doubt, the most important thing to remember in any band is the singer is the most important member. The singer is the person people come to see and hear, so what's good for the singer is good for your band. So you and the rest of your band need to listen to what the singer is doing. Know when to turn it up and when to keep it down. Listen to the narrative of the song, too. Is the song angry? Give the singer some punch. Is the song bittersweet? You might be able to linger on some of the notes. Is it a party song? Then make sure your playing makes hips swing! And whatever you do, don't make your singer struggle. Don't play unnecessarily loudly.

RIGHT: John Paul Jones is the perfect backing to legendary Led Zeppelin frontman Robert Plant.

288

Playing Bass Solos

There are a few approaches to take when it comes to playing bass solos. You can do the standard 'play it like a guitar' approach and try and cram a lot of notes in method, which can be impressive if you really know what you're doing. But what can make a bass solo special is that unlike a guitar solo, you can keep people's feet tapping while you show them what you've got. Here are a couple of approaches.

On page 292, you'll find 'Baa Baa Black Sheep' played as a fast, punky rock song.

Tip

Try starting your 'Baa Baa Black Sheep' solo along pentatonic lines.

When it comes to the solo, imagine that the song structure has been suspended, and you're free to play as you decide. Notice that the song is in G major, but only the bass drum is pulsing the beat. Don't feel shy about playing G minor pentatonic during your solo. Tease by cycling dropping to F and going up to B♭ (flat seventh and minor third). Try a minor pentatonic descent from G to G, too.

After you've tried the song, try another approach. Keep the song structure intact and try to play melodically. Try to involve arpeggios rather than playing modes and scales, making this a considered, well thought out solo. Let that inform your approach to this type of situation.

There's not a lot of call for bass solos; it's pretty cool to be able to play one, though. The bass run by Bakithi Kumalo on Paul Simon's 'You Can Call Me Al' is a particularly memorable part of a great song.

'Baa Baa Black Sheep' (Rock!)

9

Advanced Theory

We've looked at some pretty interesting scales in previous chapters. There are other scales to consider, however, and that's what this chapter is about. Now, they're pretty advanced, so there won't be anything too in-depth about them; it will suffice that for now you know what said scales are and how they're used. If you decide to take your playing further, you can investigate them. But for now, here they are.

RIGHT: Rickenbacker 4005 Lightshow (c. 1975).

294

Melodic Minor Scales

The traditional melodic minor scale shares a
flat third, as we've seen with the natural minor
scale previously. However, it has two peculiar
characteristics. If you're playing from low note
to high note (ascending), you raise the sixth and
seventh degrees of the scale. This makes it sound
like a major scale with a flatted third. If you're
playing from high note to low note, however, you
play like a natural minor.

However, in jazz usage, many players leave the scale
untouched descending. Some jazz players also use its
Lydian mode (fourth degree) to solo over dominant
seventh chords. It features a flatted seventh and a
raised fourth, giving it something of a mix between
traditional Lydian and Mixolydian modes. Therefore
it is sometimes called the Lydian flat-seven scale.

ABOVE: G melodic minor scale.

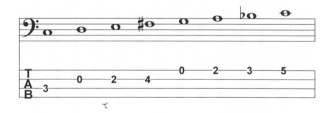

ABOVE: G Lydian flat 5.

Harmonic Minor Scale

These scales were big among the 'big hair' set during the 1980s. Partly inspired by Bach, who was big on harmonic minor scales, shred metaller and guitarist Yngwie Malmsteen used them extensively in his soloing.

The harmonic minor scale is similar to the natural minor scale, but the seventh is raised, making it just a half step below the octave. Now, that means there are three half steps between the sixth degree and the seventh degree, which generates a baroque feel. Harmonic minor scales are played the same ascending as descending.

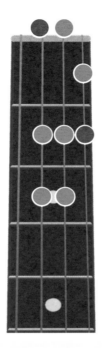

Harmonic Minor Scale

ABOVE: Notice that the A harmonic minor scale features a raised seventh note.

Harmonic & Melodic Minor Scale Modes

Both melodic and harmonic minor scales have associated modes. If you're interested, you can easily work them out for yourself. Bear in mind that both are versions of Aeolian modes, so count up three notes to find the associated Ionian mode, preserve the intervals and you have 14 new things to learn.

Chromatic Scale

Chromatic scales are composed entirely of half steps. Because of this structure, it is said to be a symmetrical scale: the same going up as coming down. Chromatic scales feature 12 notes. You'll use small parts of chromatic scales to walk to notes as previously discussed. Jaco Pastorius's composition 'Chromatic Fantasy' is an examination of chromatic scales.

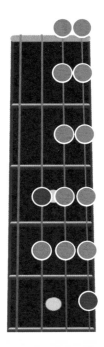

Chromatic Scale in C

ABOVE: Chromatic scales have 12 notes because they are constructed in half steps.

Whole Tone Scale

Like the chromatic scale, the whole tone scale
is symmetrical. It is composed of notes separated
entirely by whole steps. There are only six notes
in the scale, and as any triad based on a whole tone
scale will yield a raised fifth, you can attempt to use
it if you're presented with an augmented chord over
which to play.

Tip

**Some guitar players use Rimsky Korsakov's
'Flight Of The Bumblebee' to practise
their chromatic runs!**

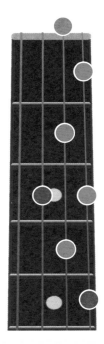

Whole Tone Scale in C

```
T                           1 — 3 — 5
A       0 — 2 — 4
B   3
```

ABOVE: Whole tone scales have just 6 notes (plus the
octave above the root) because they are constructed
in whole tone steps.

Diminished Scales

Diminished scales are also symmetrical. You can start
them from any degree and have that considered the
root of the scale, and the intervals are the same in
both directions.

There are two variations of diminished scales. One
is whole-step/half-step, the other is half-step/whole-
step. Predictably, in the former, the first interval
in the scale is a whole step, followed by a half step,
with a repeating pattern. In the latter, the interval
between the first two notes is a half step, followed
by a half between second and third, with a half
between third and fourth etc.

You can use this scale to play over diminished
seventh chords and sometimes over dominant
seventh chords to add tension. If you do this,
try to start your diminished scale half a step
above the chord's root note for best effect.

ABOVE: C whole half scale.

ABOVE: C half whole scale.

10

Other Basses

If an alien visitor asked you what an electric bass looked like, you would probably have a stock answer. You would mention four strings, frets, a pick up or two, some knobs, etc. But, the electric bass is actually a many and varied thing, with many peculiar shapes and string combinations, some stretching beyond 10 strings, frets, no frets, semi-acoustic, some upright and so on. This chapter aims to provide an overview of as many of these variations as possible: just when you think you've seen it all, something else comes along and wows you.

RIGHT: E-Gitarre Fender Jazz Bass Copy (c. 2004).

Five-String Bass

You've probably seen loads of people playing five-string bass. Most five-string basses include a low B, to achieve that extra bottom, though some use a high C if they're known for soloing. All the fingering patterns in this book will work for five-string basses tuned to low B as well as four-string basses.

Five-string basses are very popular with gospel, R&B and jazz players in particular, enabling the player to underline various phrases by dipping below low E, and to good effect.

If you're serious about your bass playing, it's not a bad idea to investigate the five-string bass. For sessions or for playing with musical productions, you'll likely be asked about whether you have one. It's a similar story if you're hoping to play in bands specializing in any of the above genres.

308

1
2
3
4
5
6
7
8
9
10
11
12

Six-String Bass

In the early days of electric bass, there were companies that designed six-string basses tuned just like guitars. These days, your tuning is more likely to be B, E, A, D, G, C. They're pretty unusual and are more often the domain of jazz and Latin bass players who need to dip to low B and solo in the high ranges.

In terms of rock music, the most high-profile six-string bass player around is Les Claypool of the band Primus and Oysterhead. His basses also tend to be fretless, and as he uses a great deal of slap and chording. He gets an incredibly distinctive sound.

If you do feel the urge to play six-string, the fingering patterns in this book will be just as applicable.

1
2
3
4
5
6
7
8
9
10
11
12

Fretless Bass

According to legend, the late bassist Jaco Pastorius had a peculiar brainwave while sitting at the back of a tour bus one day. He decided to pull all the frets out of the neck of his Fender Jazz bass with the help of a pair of pliers, thus creating the world's first fretless electric bass.

In truth, fretless basses had been around before Jaco, but he was certainly the highest profile exponent of fretless bass playing. A bass without frets enables a range of expression not possible with a fretted bass. There's a distinctive buzz derived from the metal string on a wooden fretboard, not to mention the possibility of very subtle vibrato and smooth glissando (sliding between notes). The intonation of the notes is slightly different too, enabling playing to be less exact and more expressive. That does, however, provide greater scope for slack intonation.

In the 1980s, fretless bass was all the rage: Sting used one on many early Police tours, while studio whiz Pino Palladino's work with Paul Young among others was very high profile. Jeff Ament, of Pearl Jam in the early 1990s, also used fretless bass on many recordings. These days, fretless bass is less prominent in pop and rock playing.

Eight-String & 12-String Basses

Eight-string basses differ from four-string basses in one way. Next to each string, there is a thinner string tuned one octave higher. As a result, eight-string basses sound a bit more 'guitarish' than standard basses.

The 12-string bass is similar. Next to each string, there are two thinner strings tuned in unison one octave higher.

314

This really makes a huge difference to the sound. You get the low 'oomph' of the standard bass strings, plus a chiming, almost mandolinish sound from the higher notes. Pearl Jam bassist Jeff Ament's introduction and bass line to the song 'Jeremy' is a perfect illustration. Cheap Trick bass player Tom Petersson often uses a 12-string bass, as does Doug Pinnick of King's X. Certainly in the case of Pinnick, as King's X is a power trio, the bass enables him to play simultaneously as bassist and rhythm guitarist. Try listening to their song 'Dogman'.

Electro-Acoustic Basses

There are always times when you wish you could
have an acoustic counterpart to your electric bass,
that was lightweight, you could hear without an
amp, and you could practice with.

Electro-acoustic basses are just that. They look
similar to acoustic guitars, just a bit longer and
with fewer strings. Most will also feature something
called a piezo pickup, too. Piezo pickups are
placed under the instrument's bridge and
convert changing pressure of vibrating strings
into electricity, in contrast to magnetic pickups
as discussed earlier.

Electro-acoustic basses aren't as loud as acoustic
guitars when unamplified, but if you plug them in,
you'll have no trouble. However, they sometimes
share a disadvantage with all amplified acoustic

316

instruments: they may feed back if you turn
up the volume very loud. Thus, they're best kept
for more intimate surroundings, unless, of course,
you have a fabulous sound engineer.

Are they worth buying? If you play with a lot of
acoustic guitar musicians, you're hoping to busk,
or you're planning on playing a lot of intimate
settings (restaurants for example) where you'd
rather not tote lots of heavy equipment, well then,
you can't go wrong. Try out a few at your local bass
outlet to make up your mind.

Electric Upright
Basses

Upright doesn't only refer to traditional double
basses, or as they say in some parts of the US, the
bass fiddle. Several companies sell electric basses
that are played similarly to double basses but are

318

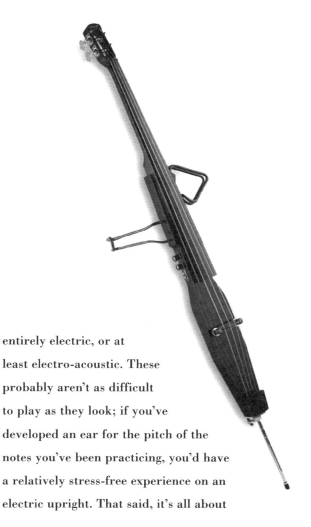

entirely electric, or at
least electro-acoustic. These
probably aren't as difficult
to play as they look; if you've
developed an ear for the pitch of the
notes you've been practicing, you'd have
a relatively stress-free experience on an
electric upright. That said, it's all about

10

what style you're planning to play. If you're thinking of moving onto a real double bass at some point in your bass life, then this will prepare you at a fraction of the price, and they're endlessly more portable.

Be warned, though, double bass strings, which you may need for your instrument, are very expensive. If that's an issue, seek out one that will take standard long gauge electric bass strings.

One Last Thing: The Chapman Stick

If you watch some Peter Gabriel live videos, you may see a tall, bald man playing a peculiar bass instrument resembling a wide, flat fretboard with two hands. The man is called Tony Levin, and the instrument is called a Chapman Stick.

It was invented by a guitarist called Emmett Chapman back in the early 1970s, and it enables you to fret bass notes and guitar-range melody notes simultaneously by tapping on the fretboard two-handed.

The standard instrument features 10 strings: five bass and five melodies. The bass strings are tuned a fourth apart while those at the melody end are a fifth apart. There is a range of tunings available. Should you invest in one? Well, only if you're planning on becoming a 'stickist'. It's a whole different instrument so if you're only planning to use it to play bass, stick with the bass. We'll let you know if we publish a *How to Play Chapman Stick* book.

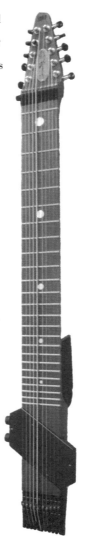

11

Fingering Guide: Scales, Modes & Arpeggios

One of the great advantages of playing the bass guitar is that once you've learned a few scale and arpeggio shapes in one key you can apply them across all the keys. Use this section as a basic source of such fingering shapes – up and down the fretboard – and you'll soon be able to play along with any combination of chords.

RIGHT: Gibson Tobias Growler (c. 2006).

322

1
2
3
4
5
6
7
8
9
10
11
12

Fingering For
Scales & Modes

As we have seen earlier, a clear understanding of
how scales and modes work, combined with a solid
knowledge of the fretboard notes will allow you to
play in a range of keys and musical styles. The
pages that follow contain all the scales and modes
you're likely to need when playing in any band: most
bassists only cover four or five of the most obvious

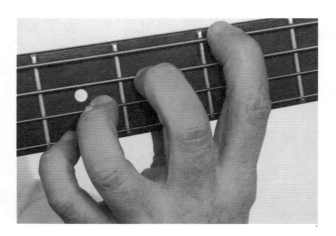

scales, but expanding your knowledge will significantly improve your ability and your enjoyment.

These pages are organized by scale or mode and give examples in two keys, two octaves for each. You will quickly see that you can use the fingering shapes in a range of keys, but to help you we've also provide the interval spelling so that you can check that your ear and fingers are working well!

Diagram Key

● These are the root notes

● These are the other notes in the scale

Intervals Key

S = semitone or half step

T = tone or whole step

$m3$ = minor third (three semitones)

$a2$ = augmented semitone (also three semitones)

11

Major Scale Fingerings

These fingerings can be applied to any major scale in any key on the electric bass. Where possible, you should also try to play all the notes of a major scale on one string. Try using these fingerings opposiste

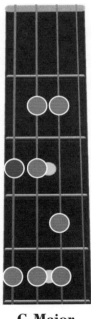

G Major

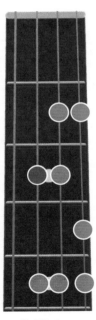

C Major

Intervals
T T S T T T S

when playing the E major scales starting at the open string. They can also be applied to the A major scales starting at open A.

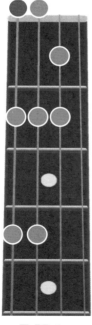

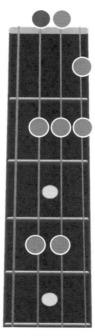

E Major

A Major

Major Pentatonic Scale

Become very familiar with major pentatonic scales over one and two octaves. The fingering is described in the following charts.

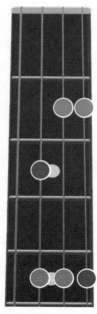

C Major Pentatonic

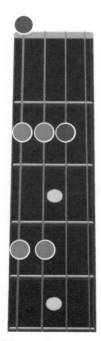

E Major Pentatonic

Intervals
T T m3 T m3

Suggested Second Octave Fingering

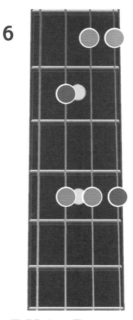

7 — C Major Pentatonic

6 — E Major Pentatonic

329

Lydian Mode

One of the lesser used modes, it's very handy to learn nevertheless.

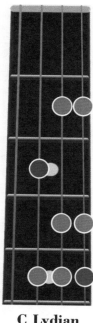

C Lydian

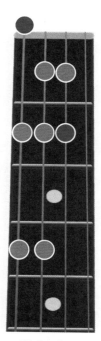

E Lydian

Intervals
T T T S T T S

Suggested Second Octave Fingering

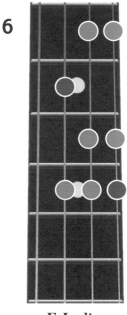

7 C Lydian

6 E Lydian

11

Natural Minor Scale (Aeolian)

The following fingerings can be applied to any natural minor scale in any key. Again, try your own version of playing the notes on just one or two strings.

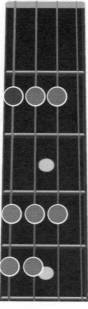

F♯ Minor

B Minor

Intervals
T S T T S T T

Try this fingering for E and A natural minor scales
starting at the open strings.

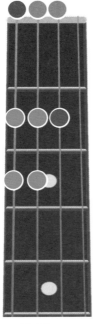

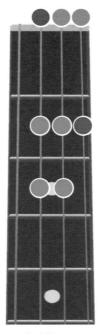

E Minor   **A Minor**

Harmonic Minor Scale

The harmonic minor is very much like a natural minor, except it uses a raised seventh.

C Harmonic Minor

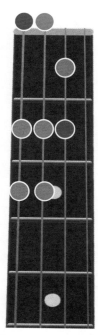

E Harmonic Minor

Intervals
T S T T S a2 S

Suggested Second Octave Fingering

7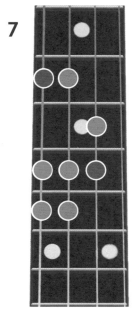

6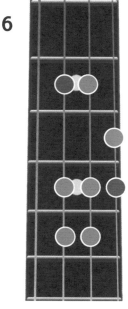

C Harmonic Minor   **E Harmonic Minor**

Melodic Minor Scale

In practice, the melodic minor scale looks very much like a major scale with a flattened third. The diagrams below show the ascending scale only.

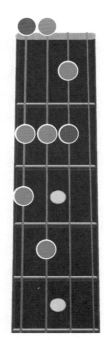

C Melodic Minor   **E Melodic Minor**

Intervals
T S T T T T S

Suggested Second Octave Fingering

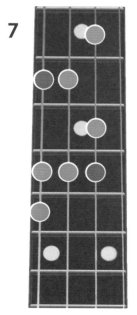

C Melodic Minor

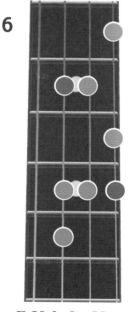

E Melodic Minor

Dorian Mode

Use these charts to play the Dorian mode, or a major scale starting at the second degree.

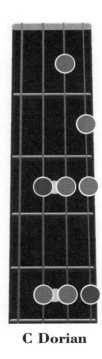

C Dorian

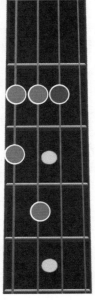

E Dorian

Intervals
T S T T T S T

Suggested Second Octave Fingering

7
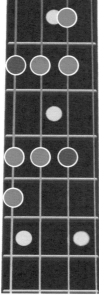

C Dorian

6
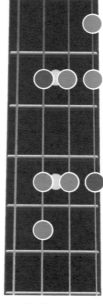

E Dorian

11

Minor Pentatonic Scale

The minor pentatonic scale is one of the most important for bass players. Use any of the following fingerings.

C Minor Pentatonic

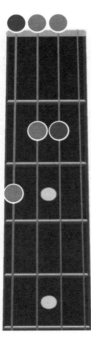

E Minor Pentatonic

Intervals
m3 T T m3 T

Suggested Second Octave Fingering

7

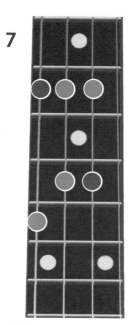

6

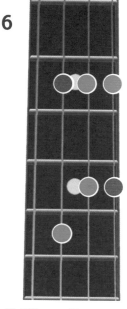

C Minor Pentatonic   E Minor Pentatonic

Blues Scale

Very similar to the minor pentatonic scale, the blues scale features an additional note, a flatted fifth.

C Blues Scale

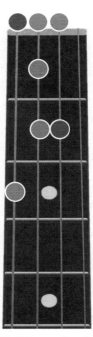

E Blues Scale

Intervals
m3 T S S m3 T

Suggested Second Octave Fingering

7
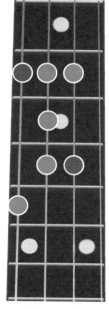

C Blues Scale

6
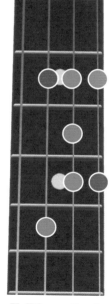

E Blues Scale

Phrygian Mode

The spaced-out sound of the Phrygian mode is great for composition on the bass.

C Phrygian

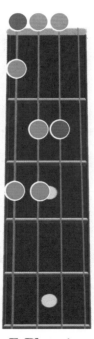

E Phrygian

Intervals
S T T T S T T

Suggested Second Octave Fingering

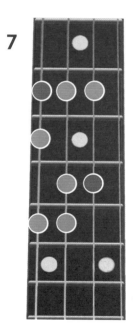

7

C Phrygian

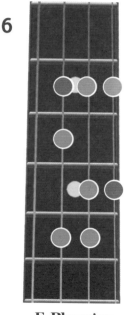

6

E Phrygian

Locrian Mode

Lesser used, but incredibly interesting, using the
Locrian mode can spice up your bass playing.

C Locrian

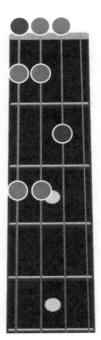

E Locrian

Intervals
S T T S T T T

Suggested Second Octave Fingering

7
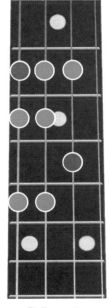

6
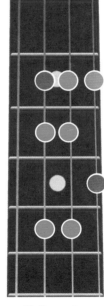

C Locrian   **E Locrian**

Half Diminished Scale

This scale is fairly specialized, but it's good to be able to understand it.

C Half Diminished

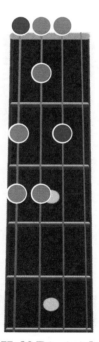

E Half Diminished

Intervals
T S T S T T T

Suggested Second Octave Fingering

7

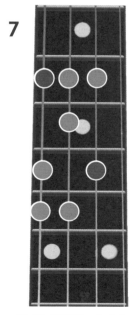

C Half Diminished

6

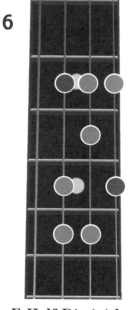

E Half Diminished

Mixolydian Mode

This is one of the fundamental modes, so it is important to know. Note also its relation to the dominant seventh chord.

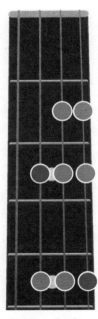

C Mixolydian

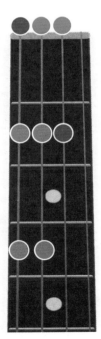

E Mixolydian

Intervals
T T S T T S T

Suggested Second Octave Fingering

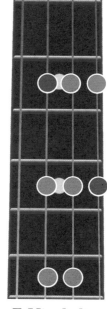

7   **6**

C Mixolydian   E Mixolydian

Chromatic Scale

Often heard in experimental music this can be used
in any key because it contains all 12 semitones.

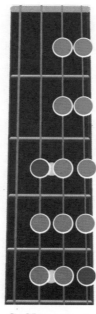

C Chromatic

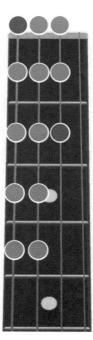

E Chromatic

Intervals

S S S S S S S S S S S

Suggested Second Octave Fingering

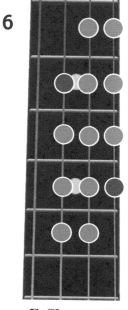

7   C Chromatic   **6**   E Chromatic

11

Whole Tone Scale

There's very little call for this scale in standard pop
music, but you can apply it if you're presented with
a diminished chord.

C Whole Tone

E Whole Tone

Intervals
T T T T T

Suggested Second Octave Fingering

7

C Whole Tone

6

E Whole Tone

Whole Step/Half Step Scales

Used more often in jazz than in rock or pop music, the whole step/half step and half step/whole step scales are played as follows.

 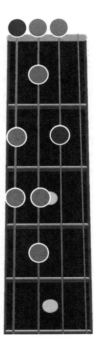

C   Whole Step/Half Step   E

Intervals
T S T S T S T S

Suggested Second Octave Fingering

7 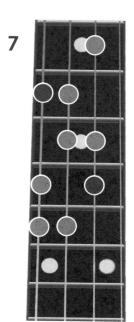 **6**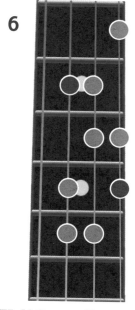

C   Whole Step/Half Step   E

11

Half Step/Whole Step Scales

Used more often in jazz than in rock or pop music,
the whole step/half step and half step/whole step
scales are played as follows.

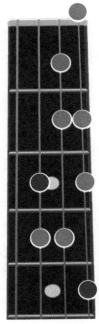 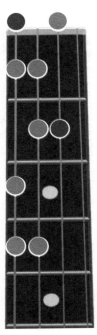

C   Half Step/Whole Step   E

Intervals
S T S T S T S T

Suggested Second Octave Fingering

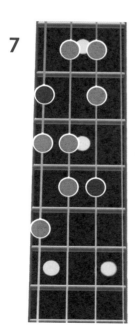

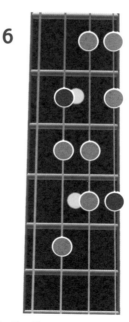

C   Half Step/Whole Step   E

Fingering For
Basic Arpeggios

Arpeggios are the cornerstone for any bass player.
While a six-string rhythm guitarist can chop away
at chords, using inversions and triads, the bassist
needs to play each note seperately, often in sync
with the bass drum. Such playing is often not flashy
but without it most songs would sound hollow and
lack impact. Arpeggios are the route to playing more
interesting bass lines, especially if you understand

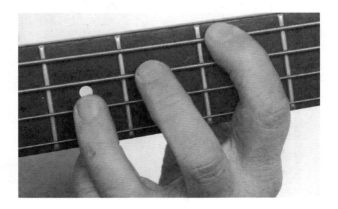

how to play all the way up the neck, using the
different fingerings for higher octaves as shown
in the following pages.

Just a few basic arpeggios are laid out here, with
just two keys and two octaves each. You can apply
the arpeggio shapes from these two keys, to all of the
others, as long as you know the notes for each fret.

To help you work out the arpeggios for each key,
a Chord spelling box is provided (the example
below is for a Major Seventh arpeggio).

Chord Notes
Root • 3rd • 5th • major 7th

Diagram Key

● These are the root notes
● These are the other notes in the scale

Major Seventh Arpeggio

These fingerings can be used for the major seventh arpeggio in any key. Make sure you think about each note you're playing and call the note names out aloud.

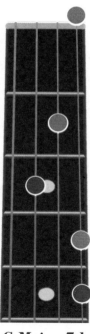

C Major 7th

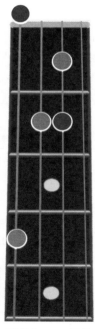

E Major 7th

Chord Notes

Root • 3rd • 5th • major 7th

Suggested Second Octave Arpeggio

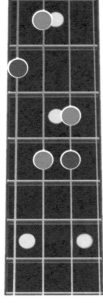

7

C Major 7th

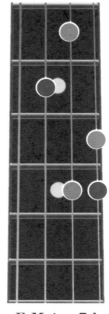

6

E Major 7th

11

Minor Seventh Arpeggio

Use these fingerings for minor seventh arpeggios.
Again, call or sing out the notes as you play them.
Try coming up with your own variations, too.

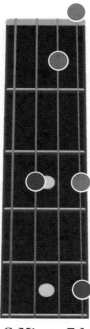 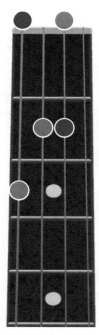

C Minor 7th   E Minor 7th

Chord Notes

Root • minor 3rd • 5th • minor 7th

Suggested Second Octave Arpeggio

7

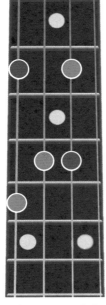

6

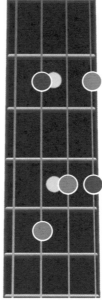

C Minor 7th

E Minor 7th

11

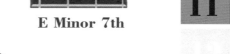

Dominant Seventh Arpeggio

Use these fingering eamples to create dominant
seventh arpeggios in each key.

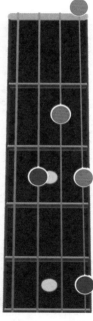

C Dom 7th

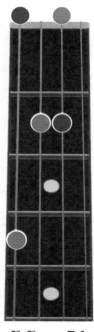

E Dom 7th

Chord Notes

Root • 3rd • 5th • minor 7th

Suggested Second Octave Arpeggio

7

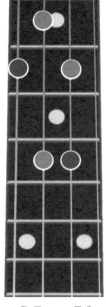

C Dom 7th

6

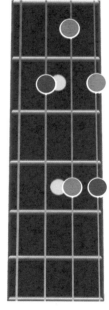

E Dom 7th

Minor 7 Flat 5
(Half Diminished Arpeggio)

This arpeggio is fairly specialized, but it's good to be able to understand it.

C Minor 7 flat 5

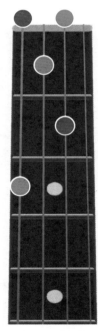

E Minor 7 flat 5

Chord Notes

Root • minor 3rd • ♭5th • minor 7th

Suggested Second Octave Arpeggio

6
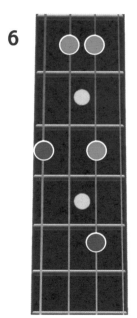

6
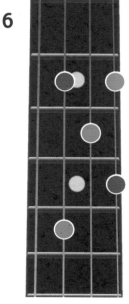

C Minor 7 flat 5   E Minor 7 flat 5

11

Diminished Chord Arpeggio

Again, a specialized arpeggio, but should it appear,
the following fingerings can be used.

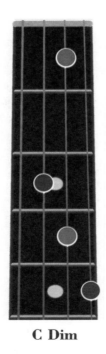

C Dim

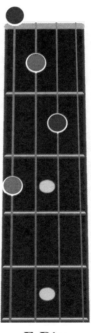

E Dim

Chord Notes

Root • minor 3rd • ♭5th

Suggested Second Octave Arpeggio

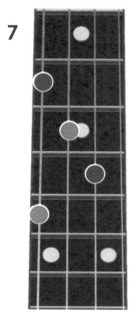

7

C Dim

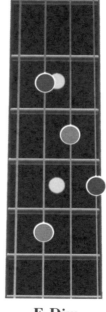

6

E Dim

11

Augmented Chord Arpeggio

This is simply a standard triad with a raised fifth (rather than a perfect fifth).

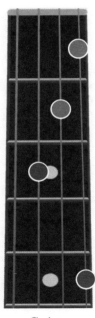

C Aug

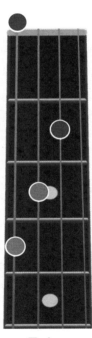

E Aug

Chord Notes

Root • 3rd • #5th

Suggested Second Octave Arpeggio

7

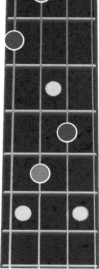

6

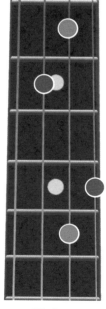

C Aug

E Aug

Ninth Arpeggio

A ninth is pretty much a dominant seventh, with the addition of a ninth, or a second played one octave higher. It is played as follows.

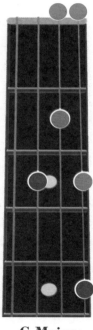

C Major

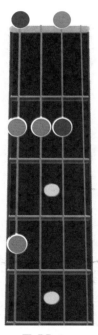

E Major

Chord Notes

Root • 3rd • 5th • minor 7th • 9th

Suggested Second Octave Arpeggio

7

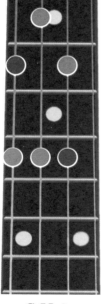

6

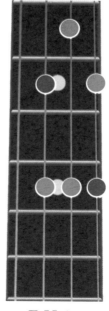

C Major   E Major

12

Resources

There are so many books, internet sites and other sources of information it is difficult to distill them down to a manageable size. However, we have provided some starting points here which can be used as a platform to search specific items of interest or more generally, for anything about music, music styles and, of course, bass playing.

1
2
3
4
5
6
7
8
9
10
11
12

RIGHT: E-Gitarre Fender Jazz Bass Copy (c. 2006).

376

12

Glossary

Action – The distance between the strings and the fretboard.

Amp – Amplifier. The electronic device that makes it possible for you to hear your bass.

Bridge – Situated at the bottom of the bass, it works with the nut to keep your strings suspended above the neck, and can be adjusted to correct intonation problems.

Cab – Cabinet. The box that houses speakers that play out the amplified sound of the bass.

Dominant – The fifth degree of the major scale.

Flatted – The lowering by a semitone of a note in the major scale.

Fret – A metal slat embedded into the neck of the bass that enables you to play notes.

378

Fretting hand – The hand you use to play notes on the neck. Usually your weaker hand; the left hand for a right-handed person.

Head – The amplifier.

Headstock – Area of the bass that holds the machine heads/tuning pegs.

Intonation – The accuracy with which notes are represented when played on the fretboard.

Major scale/chord – A scale/chord that features a root and third that are two tones apart, as well as a perfect fifth.

Minor scale – A scale/chord featuring a root and third that are a tone and a semitone apart as well as a perfect fifth.

Nut – The grooved block next to the headstock keeps the strings raised above the fretboard.

Perfect fifth – The interval of seven semitones between root and fifth.

12

Pickup – Assembly that converts the energy of the vibrating strings into electricity. Active pickups are battery powered and can add energy to the signal, while passive pickups can only regulate the power already in the circuit.

Pot – Potentiometer. A control knob on the bass that regulates volume or tone.

Signal – The current between the electric bass and the amplifier.

Signal processor – Hardware that alters the natural sound of the bass.

Subdominant – The fourth degree of the major scale.

Truss rod – Metal rod that keeps the bass neck in the correct shape.

Watt – The unit of measuring the sound output of an amplifier.

Recommended Listening

Besides songs previously mentioned, it's worth listening to the following:

'Bullet In The Head'
by Rage Against The Machine

Bassist Tim Commerford creates an unstoppable riff. In addition, the purity of the recording is an argument against the use of excessive compression.

'CB 200' by Dillinger

Chances are that the bass player on this track was either Lloyd Parks or Robbie Shakespeare. Whoever it is it is a master class in laying down an old-school reggae groove.

'Delta-V' by Squarepusher

Experimental bass player Tom Jenkinson solos with the bass, distorting it like a guitar while keeping the bottom end oomph securely in place.

'Gigantic' by The Pixies

Bassist Kim Deal keeps it foolishly simple and unadorned and as a result, the bass track on this record is incredibly suspenseful.

'Knock On Wood' by Eddie Floyd

Bass player Donald 'Duck' Dunn drives the song with power and grace via slow moving major pentatonic groove.

'Ology' by Living Colour

Bass player Muzz Skillings explores bass via harmonics, fretless playing, tone variations and looping technology.

'Pull Up To The Bumper' by Grace Jones

Robbie Shakespeare creates a bass groove with a solid bass line, a subtle slap and pop and a tasty breakdown.

'Sweet Emotion' by Aerosmith

Bass player Tom Hamilton proves that hard rock can swing and groove.

'Taxman' by The Beatles

Paul McCartney fires off a wonderful riff and executes a series of wonderful fills during the middle eight. It is an oft-copied bass line.

'School Daze' by Stanley Clarke

Clarke chords, solos, slaps and pops, combining rock and jazz fusion.

'The Spirit Of The Radio' by Rush

Bass player Geddy Lee plants a crafty flatted third and a fourth into a major pentatonic scale to create a simple foolishly memorable rock riff.

'You Keep Me Hangin' On' by The Supremes

Pretty much the entire bass output of Motown during the 1960s was played by the late great James Jamerson. This track features subtle yet complex pop bass playing that influenced nearly all his contemporaries. The Beatles 'Got To Get You Into My Life' is a sort of Paul McCartney tribute to James Jamerson.

Online Resources

www.bandmix.co.uk: A great place to find musicians if you're trying to join a band.

www.bassplayer.com: *Bass Player* magazine. An industry leading print resource for aspiring bass players and established professionals.

www.computermusic.co.uk: *Computer Music* magazine. An excellent print title to help you to learn how to make home recordings.

www.harmony-central.com: A community for musicians including lessons, news and advice.

www.spotify.com: Thousands upon thousands of tracks you can stream to your computer free of charge. If you're not sure how something sounds, you can search for it here. It has limitations, but it's definitely worth trying out for aspiring bass players. Most tracks in this book can be found there.

www.youtube.com: It goes without saying, but if you want to find out how something sounds, or what an old bass player looked like, it's your first port of call.